The History of Radley

by

Patrick Drysdale, Rita Ford, Patricia Groser, Marian Orchard, Ann Parkes, Kay Williams

Original drawings by Jim Webb

Radley History Club
2002

To the memory of

Joy Alexander,

founder of the Radley History Club

and originator of this book

Edited and designed by Patrick Drysdale

ISBN 0-9542761-0-8

Published by Radley History Club
PO Box 169, Abingdon, OX14 3WZ

Printed and bound in Great Britain
by Biddles Ltd, *www.biddles.co.uk*

Contents

Illustrations

Acknowledgements

Although six members of the Radley History Club are listed as authors of this book, invaluable help in research and preparation of some chapters was given by other members, including Heather Calvert-Fisher, Penelope Clark, Anne Hayton, Doug and June Rawlinson, Mary Shayler and Rosemary Stafford. Other members, including David Buckle, Jean Deller, and John Homewood, provided valuable information in reply to questions. Jean Deller was especially helpful in lending pictures for illustrations, and Doug Rawlinson generously allowed us to reproduce slides from his large collection of Radley photographs. John Orchard gave computer help and took several photographs as sources for drawings. Thanks are due also to Joan Gibbs and Stanley Baker for their proofreading of the manuscript and to the latter for his painstaking work on the pictures and in the preparation of the Bibliography and the Index. He also supplied some of the photographs.

Beyond the Club, a number of people have provided information and responded to queries, among them J. Peter Brown, Charles Graves, Ruth Poirette Gordon, W.C. Grimes and Michael Prince. Mieneke Cox gave encouragement at the beginning and helpful guidance on our approach to the sixteenth century.

Particular thanks go to Tony Money, Archivist of Radley College, for allowing generous access to the collection of papers there and for providing photographs for illustrations. The authors are also grateful for help from the staffs of the Berkshire Records Office, the Centre for Oxfordshire Studies at the Oxford Central Library, and the Local Studies section of Abingdon Public Library.

The maps on the front cover and on page 88 are reproduced from Ordnance Survey mapping on behalf of The Controller of Her Majesty's Stationery Office © Crown Copyright. MC100037741.

Foreword

In the early stages of the preparation of this book it was necessary for the authors to define what we meant by 'Radley' in the title. To limit ourselves to the present boundaries of the civil parish, as set out in the changes of 1986, would have been unrealistic since much of the story of Radley farming, for example, involves land that is now part of Abingdon. Going further back, to the Middle Ages, Radley must have been a small hamlet without known boundaries, a tiny part of the huge Barton estate of Abingdon Abbey. Even earlier, going back to Neolithic times and before, there were people here before there were any fixed boundaries. So it was decided that the book must be in general terms about the Radley area; in practice this means roughly the area within the pre-1986 boundaries of the civil parish, and so it includes the former sites of Barton and Barton Court Farm in the southwest as well as the modern Audlett Drive and Peachcroft estates.

A far greater problem was posed by the huge gaps in the evidence. While twentieth-century excavations have told us much about Neolithic, Bronze Age, and Iron Age settlements in the area, as well as about Romans and Saxons, there is no specific mention of Radley in the surviving records of Abingdon Abbey until the late twelfth century. Again, there are few specific references to the name between then and the late sixteenth century. In many cases, therefore, we have had to write in terms of general rather than purely local history and to make assumptions about what was happening in our village and its surrounding area on the basis of what was happening elsewhere in the country. Even after the sixteenth century, despite the fact that there is much more evidence of what was happening in Radley, we have still from time to time had to make reference to trends and movements in the country as a whole.

The authors, therefore, are well aware that some readers will wish there was more information specifically about Radley. We must even agree with those readers. In fact, it must be emphasized that we make no claim to closure or completeness, for we know that no history is ever final and that there must always be more that could be said and more that will one day be discovered. We can even say that we hope we have opened up the subject of Radley history to further research and insights on the part of others. On the other hand, we hope that we have fulfilled our two main purposes, to write an interesting and informative book and to unfold the various stages by which the Radley area has arrived at what it is today.

Chapter 1

Ancient Times

Introduction and Geology

The Upper Thames valley largely assumed its present-day form during the Pleistoscene (Ice Ages) period, beginning about 2 million years ago. During the great climatic changes of its bitterly cold glaciations separated by periods of warmth, the weight of the ice and the freezing and thawing of the ground caused great masses of earth and rock debris to be carried into the valley, where they were laid down as gravel terraces. Incorporated within the gravels, especially during the later periods, are the flint tools lost or discarded by early man in the area. While some tools appear quite fresh, others are smoothed and rounded in various degrees from being rolled and transported in the gravels in which they are found. Also within the gravels are found the bones of the animals with which early man shared the valley – woolly mammoth, rhinoceros, giant deer, elephant and wild ox. There are four gravel terraces correlating with the ends of the four Ice Ages. The size of the gravel or sand particles indicates the rate of flow of the river. Various bands of fine sand to coarse gravel can be seen in most gravel pits. The oldest terraces are the highest, the younger ones being laid down at lower levels as the river cut downwards. 'Drift' is the detritus and boulder clay left behind by the ice. Deposition still occurs today in the valley floor. This most recent deposit is the alluvium, fine particles carried by the river, which give the muddy colour when floods occur. Although a layer of less than a millimetre in thickness may be left behind, over several hundred years an appreciable thickness can accumulate.

During the twentieth century in the Radley area Terrace 1 and parts of Terrace 2, the younger terraces, have been widely quarried for the gravels that cover the Kimmeridge clay. As a result, some of the very earliest history of the area has been pieced together from artefacts found during quarrying or investigations prior to gravel extraction.

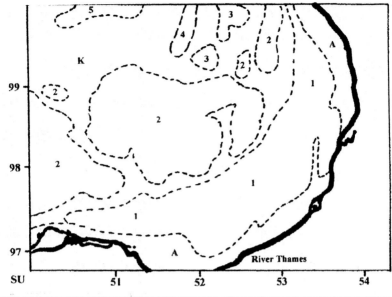

A	Youngest	Alluvium	
1		First Terrace	Floodplain Terrace
2		Second Terrace	Summertown-Radley Terrace
3		Third Terrace	Wolvercote Terrace
4		Fourth Terrace	Handborough Terrace
5		Plateau Drift	Not Strictly a Terrace
K		Kimmeridge Clay	

1:1. Schematic map of the gravel terraces at Radley.

At Radley isolated patches on hill summits can be correlated with Terrace 4. Radley Church is on a small area of Terrace 3. Lower Radley, Thrupp, and Pumney are on Terrace 1, and the bulk of the modern village is on Terrace 2 (Jarvis, p. 7).

The Plateau Drift is the oldest geology of the Radley area, dating from around a million years ago. It occurs in patches around Sugworth (Goudie & Hart, p. 5) and was exposed at Sugworth Lane during excavations for the A34 By-pass. Amongst smaller fauna remains were found those of the extinct Etruscan rhinoceros. Also found here were samples of pollen from ancient pine trees, causing their location to be recognized as a Site of Special Scientific Interest.

In a gravel pit called Sylvester's Pit, near Gooseacre Farm, which is situated on the second gravel terrace, remains have been found of horse, ox, hippopotamus, stag and part of the upper jaw of a cave lion.

The thighbone of a mammoth, which had sunk into the clay, was found while digging the foundations of a new house (at Radley College) from the overlying fourth gravel terrace (Huntingford, p. 151).

Nature had provided Radley with river access, plenty of springs, easy to work gravels, wood, animals and fish. The scene was set for man to move into the area.

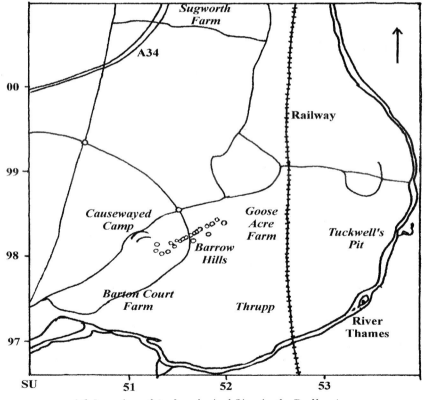

1:2 Location of Archaeological Sites in the Radley Area.

Palaeolithic Man

The Neanderthal, Palaeolithic / Old Stone Age people of more than 30,000 years ago were not anatomically modern humans like we are today but an early type of people who are now extinct. These nomadic hunter-gatherers lived on the edge of the forests, dressed in animal skins, and crossed and re-crossed the terrain foraging for plants and fruits and hunting wild animals.

A very rare Mousterian-type flint hand-axe dating from this period was found on the underlying Kimmeridge clay after gravel extraction at Tuckwell's Pit (Tyldesly, p.149). This does not mean that early Stone Age man stood at that point, since all the gravel terraces were moved during their formation by river action, but it is evidence that he was in the area. Other Palaeolithic stone and flint remains from over 10,000 years ago have been found in the Thrupp area.

Mesolithic Remains

Mesolithic/ Middle Stone Age man (8000-4000 B.C.), dating from the end of the last Ice Age, was also a hunter-gatherer. At this time the Thames valley would have still been largely wooded with human activity taking place on the forest margins. Mesolithic flint work has been recovered near Gooseacre Farm, near Thrupp Farm, and from south of Pumney Farm.

Although deep ploughing had damaged the site, a Mesolithic hut circle excavated at Thrupp revealed primitive flint tools and weapons (Holgate, p.6). A Mesolithic quartzite hand-axe probably used for cutting and scraping was found at Thrupp and also a Mesolithic pick, one of a new type of tool dating from this period. Mesolithic tools are commonly found close to rivers, suggesting the people lived along riverbanks and used water for transport.

Up until this time the land bridge between Britain and the Continent still existed. It disappeared about 6500 B.C., but developments from more advanced cultures still spread to our island.

The Neolithic Age

With the arrival around 4000 B.C. of Neolithic (New Stone Age) man, the landscape began to change. The Neolithic introduction of farming brought to an end the slow development of the hunter-gatherers and initiated a time of rapid change. The farmers used their flint axes to clear forests and had primitive ploughs and digging sticks with which to prepare the ground for wheat and barley. Domestic animals were kept, even though hunting was still important. From what is known about Neolithic domestic sites in Britain, they consisted of timber houses with shallow foundations and internal hearths; these dwellings were surrounded by pits, working areas and middens (refuse heaps near dwellings). Pottery pots were used for cooking.

Later Neolithic occupation is conspicuous at Thrupp Farm, where burials have been found on different sites (SU 5228 9714 and SU 523 973), and at Barton Court Farm. Neolithic finds in the Radley area are prolific and sites include a causewayed enclosure at Pond Head (SU 511 982), domestic site/sites at Thrupp, and the earlier development of the Barrow Hills site.

The Neolithic causewayed enclosure stood on a small spur bounded by the valleys of two streams, which ran to the Thames. The enclosure consisted of inner and outer ditches, the former with a raised track (causeway) and the latter possibly so. There is a suggestion there may even have been a third ditch but development of the area precludes further investigation. The ditches extended in arcs between the two small valleys. The distribution of late Neolithic and early Bronze Age ring ditches nearby at Barrow Hills suggests that the enclosure may have lain by a track running to the south, aligned south-east to north-west, more or less along the line of the second gravel terrace. The main archaeological site was discovered as early as 1926 but the outer ditch was not discovered until 1954. Further investigations took place in the 1960s prior to the building of Cameron Avenue and Gordon Drive. In the earlier period (c. 3700-3300 B.C.) the enclosure is thought to have been bounded by a low bank, possibly with a timber stockade on its crest, for keeping domestic animals in and wild animals out, enclosing about three acres. In the second period (c. 3400-2900 B.C.) the inner ditch was filled and the outer ditch was cut. The families that occupied this site not only were subsistence farmers and hunters but also had industries of flint-knapping and making bone tools and 'Abingdon Ware' pottery, which is the oldest known locally made pottery. Flint-knapping is the making or reworking of flint tools by the skilful striking of one flint stone against another to fracture off pieces of the target stone until it is suitable for the required usage. 'Grooved Ware' is a slightly more elaborate pottery, sherds of which were found with flintwork deposits in the later ditch silts (Avery1982). Excavation material from the causewayed enclosure is in the Ashmolean museum.

1:3. An 'Abingdon Ware' pot.

Nearby, cutting into one of the ditches, an early-to-middle Neolithic oval barrow was excavated in 1983 (Barclay & Halpin, pp. 19-31). Archaeologists found two crouched skeletons, male and female, buried side by side. A polished flint blade was placed with the adult female burial and a jet or shale belt-slider lay near the man's hip. An arrowhead found nearby could have been placed near the head. The shale probably came from the north of England.

Three single inhumation graves at the northwest end of the Barrow Hills complex (described below) are also dated from this period (3700 to 3100 B.C.). A pit burial of the disarticulated remains of a young adult male in an area of intercutting pits contained 24 flint blades and flakes (Barclay & Halpin, pp. 31-34). The proximity of the Barrow Hills site and the causewayed enclosure suggests that the two sites could have been in use at the same time.

The Radley Barrow Hills complex developed over a period of 3000 years from the early Neolithic through to the middle Bronze Age and covers an area of at least ten acres, centred on SU 5160 9830, on the second gravel terrace, east of the causewayed enclosure (Barclay & Halpin, p.1). The site extends for approximately one kilometre, with a linear cemetery of at least 25 barrows of Neolithic and Bronze Age date aligned WSW-ENE. It is unlikely to have extended to the SW of the enclosure since excavations at Barton Court Farm revealed only isolated Neolithic pits in this direction. The barrow forms range in diameter from 17.5 to 40 metres and include a pond barrow, a barrow with a segmented ring ditch, an oval barrow, and round barrows. There were also flat graves and pit burials and cremations. The site is recognized as a nationally important site with many finds, now not only in local museums and the Oxford Ashmolean Museum but also with a wealth of material lodged in the British Museum. The layout of the barrows in two parallel rows, the types of the mounds and even the grave goods all reveal that Barrow Hills is a classic Wessex cemetery in exile. It's nearest counterpart geographically is the Lambourn Seven Barrows, but this cemetery has its closest links to those on Salisbury Plain.

The extent of the barrows was first revealed by aerial photography in the 1930s (Allen 1984) and they have been excavated on and off over a long period. The excavations in the 1980s were spurred on by the plans to develop large parts of the site for housing.

The overall picture of the middle Neolithic landscape around Barrow Hills is of open conditions with local woodland restricted to Daisy Bank Fen (now managed by the Berkshire, Buckinghamshire and Oxfordshire Wildlife Trust as the Abbey Fishponds Nature Reserve). Grassland probably predominated but there would also have been some cereal crops. Animal-bone remains suggest a low proportion of sheep bones, cattle and pigs being more suitable for woodland browsing/grazing. Later Neolithic remains suggest that the secondary woodland around Daisy Bank Fen had been largely cleared (Barclay & Halpin, p. 1).

Later Neolithic and Early Bronze Age (2500-2000 B.C.)

Beaker burials are associated with this period. Several Beaker burials have been recovered from the Radley area, but many were salvaged in advance of gravel extraction and precise details are scarce. A Wessex/Middle-Rhine-style beaker was found at Tuckwell's pit (SU 5318 9854) (Wallis, p.137). A Beaker burial was found during gravel extraction NE of Thrupp Farm (SU 524 977) (Ainslie 1992), and another burial was discovered close to the present-day site of 84 Lower Radley, where there were sherds of pottery with a beaded decoration (Ainslie 1987).

Beakers were deposited in 7 graves on the Barrow Hills site. Some were flat graves and some were barrows. The beaker variations (Barclay & Halpin, p. 56) ranged from a small crude vessel placed near the hand of a child, a beaker with simple decoration in a female adult grave, and, as would be expected from associated trends, larger, finer beakers in the male adult graves, including two splendid beakers with complex decoration found with rich burials (Barclay & Halpin, pp. 57, 65).

1:4. A 'Wessex/Middle Rhine' beaker from the Barrow Hills complex.

1: 5. A 'European' beaker from the Barrow Hills complex.

The child grave was unusually 'rich' for a child and contained 3 copper rings, each of which used a different technology. These are among the most interesting metallic finds from the area, partly due to a lack of parallels. They may be some of the earliest known metalwork in Britain (2700-2200 B.C.). It is not known if these rings were imports or the product of local industry. They may indicate the importance of the Thames as a means of communication not only with the adjacent areas but also with the other side of the North Sea (Barclay & Halpin, p. 327).

The beaker burial of a young male adult skeleton lying on his side with his knees bent, a beaker placed next to his head and the flint arrowhead remains of his quiver of arrows alongside, was excavated at the Barrow Hills complex. An arrowhead lodged in his back showed the cause of his death (Barclay & Halpin, p. 140). Artefacts from the grave of another male included a pair of sheet-gold basket 'ear-rings' (now thought by some to have possibly been hair ornaments) (Sherrat 1986, 1987) and two gold-foil cones/bead covers (a class of artefacts typically found in Wessex burials). These are amongst some of the oldest known British gold work and are normally on display at the Ashmolean Museum.

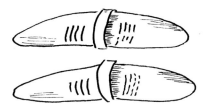

1: 6. Gold basket 'ear-rings'. Only six pairs of such 'ear-rings' have been found in Britain. They seem to belong to an insular tradition developed from continental prototypes.

Other grave goods from the beaker burials include flint arrowheads, flakes and blades, an antler spatula and a winged-head bone pin which is comparable with an example from North Saxony (Barclay & Halpin, p. 65).

Bronze Age

The Bronze Age folk – Matthew Arnold's 'Dark Iberians' – were artists, traders and craftsmen in metal. They were peaceful and hardworking people who set up small communities with circular huts and farm yards; they cultivated grain, domesticated animals, wore simple woollen clothes and buried their dead in cinerary urns as well as graves. Bronze Age settlers were widely found on the same sites as their predecessors and continued to use and develop the Barrow Hills burial site. Did the Bronze Age settlers represent conquest by peoples coming from the Continent or the adoption of the latest technology by the already settled population? It is not always clear.

Round barrows are the most common style of interment associated with this era but not all burials during this period contained beakers. Other forms of pottery have been recovered from the Barrow Hills site, including food vessels and urns. A bronze awl and flint flakes were found in a crouched burial grave. Human cremated remains in a funerary urn and various 'Grooved Ware' pottery sherds were recovered from the pond barrow, which is believed to have remained open until the Saxon period. Red-deer antlers and articulated cattle limbs were found in the segmented ring ditch.

The Bronze Age burial practices at Barrow Hills included crouched burials, inhumations, vessels containing cremated bones, a beaker containing the disarticulated bones of a new-born baby, partially articulated skeletons and wooden coffin burials. Many of the human remains did not come from the actual barrows but from pits and ditches. As well as pottery, grave goods included arrowheads, a copper/bronze awl, beads of amber, shale and faience, bone items, bronze/copper knives and daggers. However, the use of the term 'dagger' for these thin blades is misleading: they were the knife and scissors of the Bronze Age housewife. Lowly burials far outnumbered those with significant grave goods.

Some of the earlier barrows were reused in the later Bronze Age. Although the barrow complex was built up gradually over time, there appears to be an underlying pattern, possibly showing a respect for earlier burials, in their alignment and construction sequence along the crest of the gravel terrace. Some of the later barrows form an avenue along a parallel axis. Some barrows have not yet been excavated, so the Radley site still may have secrets to reveal. The organisation and dramatic spatial layout of the Radley round barrow group can be explained as a 'processional' way to a large open space at the western end (Barclay & Halpin, pp. 305-309).

Middle Bronze Age metalwork has been dredged from the River Thames between Radley and Abingdon, including a rapier and a palstave (an axe shaped to fit into a split handle). These are thought to be ritualistic gifts to humour the temperamental river gods (Thomas, pp. 246-248).

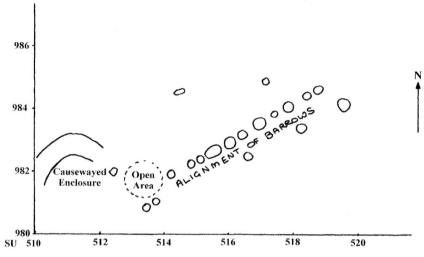

1: 7. The layout of Barrow Hills monument complex.

Iron Age

Around 800 B.C. Celtic people brought new ideas and revolutionary technology. Iron, tougher and more durable, replaced the use of bronze as the stock material for implements. Celtic society included metal workers, carpenters, herdsmen, farmers and fishermen. Celtic tribes had by this time occupied much of Europe, subduing everyone in their path, and they invaded Britain in successive waves over several hundred years. Throughout their period of dominance here, they maintained powerful links with the Continent, trading with the Mediterranean and other areas.

Later Bronze Age and early Iron Age occupation is best represented in the enclosures, fields and domestic features of Eight Acre Field (SU 525 980), two kilometres to the SE of Barrow Hills. A late Bronze Age waterhole and a small quantity of contemporary pottery were found here within a system of ditches, fields and tracks.

Iron Age remains have been found in the field to the east of Whites Lane, at the rear of Foxborough Road, not far from the Barrow Hills site (Leeds, pp. 399-404). Iron Age activity is noticeably absent from the Barrow Hills site, so the new inhabitants perhaps respected it as a cemetery.

Abingdon Area Archaeological & Historical Society has been involved in excavations at Thrupp Farm and Tuckwell's Pit (SU 523 978) (Wilson 1997; Ainslie 1992, 1993). At Thrupp an Iron Age hut circle (one of a series of occupation sites in the area) was revealed, consisting of an incomplete ring of postholes with a diameter of 29ft. An Iron Age hut would have been built of wood with a thatched roof. Three complete pots, a complete triangular loom weight and a large quantity of animal bones were identified. These bones were mainly of sheep, which is interesting in view of the general absence of sheep noted earlier. To the east of the main house was a well, the contents of which included deposits containing iron-smithing slag and parts of crucibles used for bronze casting.

Later Iron Age finds (mainly pottery sherds) have also been made at Sugworth Farm (Miles 1976, p. 6-11).

The Romans

Celtic Britain became a tempting prize to Imperial Rome, and the country had rich metallic ore deposits that were already being traded with the Romans. Julius Caesar attacked Britain in 55 and 54 B.C. Some local kings surrendered to him, and he imposed a tribute, or annual tax, payable to Rome. In 43 A.D., to subdue the threatening power of the Celts, there was a more substantial invasion under Claudius. Salway (p. 9) points out:

> But for the future of the British landscape the most interesting change is the widespread emergence, particularly in the period between Caesar and Claudius (54 B.C.-A.D. 43), of a more permanent pattern of rural land settlement, with regular boundaries that suggest regular tenure. There is a growing feeling among archaeologists that this period may mark the beginning of a framework of land-division that has persisted to the present day.

Pottery making was an extensive industry in the Oxford area in Roman times. Pots were of better quality than those previously made locally, although a few of the imported Beaker pots had been extremely fine. Settlers traded their wares and farm products, and diets became more varied with the introduction of a wider variety of vegetables and herbs. A new type of exchange – coinage – began to be used in place of traditional iron currency bars.

The Romans began to build rectangular stone buildings, whereas in the Iron Age and earlier there had been circular wooden structures. Most important, perhaps, were the Roman villas, built obviously for the more important people. An example of a small villa was at Barton Court Farm, built on the site of Neolithic, Bronze- and Iron-Age settlements. It is one of the few Romano-British settlements in the area that has been outlined. Before the area was developed for modern housing, the site around Barton Court Farm was extensively excavated and revealed a large farmstead. The main house was originally a simple rectangular building but over the centuries it gained the usual terraced corridor and also a wine cellar. A smaller building stood opposite and there were grain dryers nearby. The whole was surrounded by an elaborate maze of banks and ditches. Contents of the well included a considerable amount of good-condition ironwork (including latch-lifters, a spearhead, the well-hook and iron bucket binding). Six leather shoes were found in the well and also a large quantity of pottery with many vessels almost complete. In an area reserved for infant burial the remains of twenty-five babies were revealed, some newborn, some possibly a few weeks old. Sheep were still more abundant farm animals than cattle, while pigs and horses were less common. Carbonized seeds recovered from stratified deposits identify the farm crops to include barley, three species of wheat (spelt, emmer, and bread or club wheat), flax, Celtic bean and vetch. When the Romans left our shores, the farmstead was systematically demolished, the stone removed and the cellar filled in (Miles 1986).

In 1969 Radley College History and Archaeology Society began to investigate a gravel site patterned with crop marks, now partly covered by

Peachcroft estate. Several ditches and pits were excavated (SU 514 986) which revealed a Romano-British habitation site with a large number of postholes, which may represent one rectangular and two round huts. Most of the evidence consisted of fragments of pottery, including a few scraps of earlier Gaulish Samian ware, a carved bone knife handle, several pieces of glass and many nails. It is very likely that the buildings were a humble farmstead and most of the pottery was rough household ware. Part of a wall was revealed and a few fragments of tile packed in clay were found. The few coins found on the Peachcroft site were of late 3rd and early 4th century A.D. dates though the occupation is thought to be earlier. (*The Radleian* c. 1969-72; *Berkshire Archaeological Journal* 1970, p. 5; *Oxoniensia* 1972, p. 104).

Gooseacre is (in the official list of sites to be preserved and protected) a scheduled Romano-British settlement. Trial trench evaluations in September 1990 indicated an extensive Romano-British field arrangement in the northern half of the field (SU 525 980), and certain features suggest prehistoric occupation in the southern half.

The area of the Barrow Hills barrows appears to have been avoided for habitation in the Roman period, but some settlement and a trackway skirted the periphery of the monument complex. 'The location of two late Roman cemeteries near the upstanding barrows   may again suggest a certain degree of respect and deliberate avoidance' (Barclay & Halpin, p. 325). Forty-seven Romano-British burials, aligned north-south, have been uncovered in these cemeteries, and these graves may have been begun in the first century A.D. (Chambers, p. 24). There is no definite evidence to link this cemetery with the Barton Court villa. The 1940s excavation, which uncovered the first 35 burials (Atkinson 1952-3), revealed three graves with grave goods. One grave site had five very corroded iron nails and staining suggesting the original presence of a wooden coffin. Another grave contained a red-coloured beaker with white slip decoration, a type common in the third and fourth centuries A.D. One body had been buried with nine coins tied up in a piece of coarse linen cloth. Five of the coins

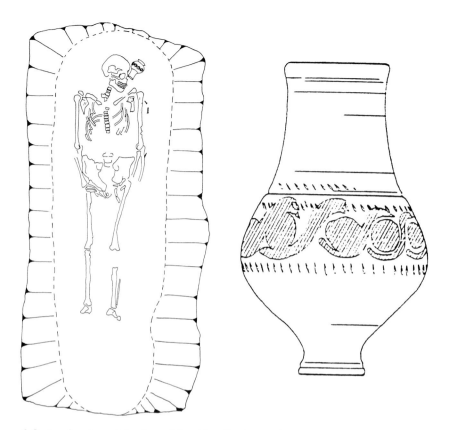

1:8. A red-coloured beaker with white slip decoration and the Roman grave in which it was found. Copyright © Oxford Archaeology.

carried London mint marks; three were from Treveri and one from Thessalonica. All were dated between 317 and 324 A.D. As early as 1880, two Roman pots were found in a field approximately half a mile north of Radley Church and opposite the entrance to Sugworth Lane.

The village of Radley boasts some remarkable and unique archaeological evidence, which has not yet revealed and may never reveal the full picture.

Chapter 2

Saxons and Normans

It is customary to say that the Romans left Britain in 410 A.D. In fact, the legions were recalled to help defend Rome in 406, and we can assume that their departure from their many outposts from the South coast to Hadrian's wall took at least four years. But these were just the legions and military governors. They left behind a Romano-British culture that had become established over four centuries and continued to exist until it was overrun by that of the Anglo-Saxons. Because of the continuity of occupation, as revealed by extensive recent archaeology, 'the Abingdon area is especially important for the study of the transition from Romano-British society to the first English communities' (Miles 1986, p. 3).

Anglo-Saxons is the name given to the Germanic peoples – Angles, Jutes and Saxons – who populated Britain in the fifth and sixth centuries. They brought with them their language, or rather a variety of West Germanic dialects, one of which, the West Saxon, later became the basis of standard southern English. The first Anglo-Saxons in England came as soldiers or servants – perhaps as slaves – of the Romans. It was not until the middle of the fifth century that they came as land-hungry armed settlers. The story in Bede's history that King Vortigern invited them to help defend Britain from the Picts and the Scots may or may not be true. However the invasions began, they lasted for about a hundred and fifty years, during which time the Romano-British were either pushed westwards or absorbed into the new society. It was during this period, early in the sixth century, that the Romano-British were rallied and heroically led by the general, real or legendary, known to us as Arthur.

The Angles mainly came to the east coast and the Jutes to what became Kent, Hampshire and the Isle of Wight. The Saxons, or many of them, came to the south coast and gradually pushed up through what became Hampshire and Berkshire until they reached the Thames. It is possible, though, that the first settlers in the Abingdon area approached up the river.

By the time the Saxons reached what became the Radley area, the villa at Barton had been 'efficiently and systematically demolished' (Miles 1974), presumably for re-erection elsewhere, possibly to be placed in a safer area within or beyond the town. Saxon settlers, however, moved onto the site quite early and built amongst the ruins (Miles 1986). A gilded saucer brooch was found when this site was excavated and also the remains of a Saxon warrior, probably of the sixth century. He was buried in a north-south alignment, so he was almost certainly a pagan.

These early Saxon settlements were quite small and often did not last long. Their houses were built by sinking postholes into the ground and filling the spaces with wattle and daub. As these buildings decayed and the adjacent arable plots were worked out, the families would move on to another site in the area, often shifting at intervals of a generation or more. The settlement at Barton seems to have been deserted quite quickly, and a much larger settlement was established in the Barrow Hills area. The Bronze Age earthworks here seem to have been respected, though a number of the monuments were reused for burial. Excavations on this site in 1983-84 found traces of more than ten post-built houses, some of which had posts set in pairs, perhaps to allow wattle panels to be stood between them. There were also forty *grubenhäuser* (earth houses, or 'sunken featured buildings'), which were dwellings or storage areas partially sunk into the

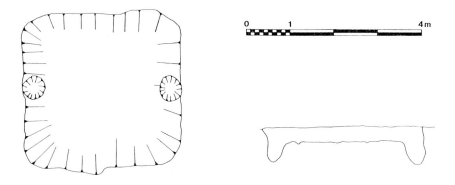

2:1. Diagram and section of a Saxon 'sunken featured building'.
Copyright © Oxford Archaeology.

ground and covered over with material built around a single central post. Finds here included bone and pottery spindle whorls, fragments of loom weights, a triangular bone comb, a copper-alloy penannular brooch and large quantities of pottery. Some of the pottery was of a type found also on the Continent (Bradley 1984). The name Barrow Hills must be of Saxon origin, though it is first recorded (as 'Barrow Hilles') in a land revenue document of 1547 (Gelling 1974). There must also have been a settlement at Sugworth, where a Saxon farm was revealed in 1972 (Miles 1976). The name Sugworth is first recorded in Domesday and comes from *Sugoarde*, 'Sucga's yard (or enclosure)', while neighbouring Sunningwell means 'the well of the Suningas'.

During the seventh and eighth centuries there was a great deal of fighting between rival groups of Anglo-Saxons, and towards the end of this period control of the northern part of what became Berkshire alternated between the kingdoms of Wessex and Mercia. (Wessex was based in Winchester but then went westward only as far as part of Dorset, while Mercia by then covered most of central and eastern and some of northern England.) In fact, from 779 onwards Berkshire was part of Mercia, perhaps for some seventy years (Stenton 1913). To what extent these struggles affected the community at Barton, for example, or the larger community at Abingdon, we do not know. Finally Wessex restored its supremacy and then, under Alfred the Great, became the dominant kingdom of England. By this time the main enemy were the Danes, who had occupied Northumbria (which lay north of the Humber) and Anglia as well as Mercia. Alfred fought them successfully, after a few setbacks, and agreed boundaries with them. Later they and the Scots were decisively defeated in 937 by Athelstan (895-939), King of Wessex from 925 and of England from 926.

Alfred may have been born at Wantage and is said to have built a royal residence either there or at Abingdon. He was responsible for a period of stability in England and also for the spread, or revival, of learning. He arranged for the translation from Latin of the Venerable Bede's

Ecclesiastical History of the English People (A.D. 731) and other important texts, and he set up a new system of laws.

Up until then learning had been kept alive by the Church, especially in the monasteries and abbeys that grew up during the early Saxon period. Bede himself was a monk at Jarrow, in what is now Tyne and Wear. Celtic Christianity had flourished in parts of England during the Roman period, and it was brought from Ireland to Iona in the north by St. Columba in 563, but the religion was apparently brought to the pagan Anglo-Saxons first by St. Augustine, who landed in Kent in 597. In 635 the first West Saxon bishopric was founded at Dorchester, though this later came under the control of Mercia, and in 675 there began the series of events that led to the foundation of Abingdon Abbey. Lands for the establishment of a monastery were granted to a minor lord called Hean and his sister Cissa. The building was to be on the Hill of Abbun, which is thought to have been in the Boars Hill area, above Chilswell and Henwood (Cox 1986, p. 75). It seems that little or no building was done here, and in 685 Cadwalla, who was then King of Wessex, gave Hean and Cissa a large tract of land, the royal vill of Sevekesham, which was thereafter to be called Abbendune. Here, at or near the site of the present abbey ruins, a monastery was built a little before or after 700, and it became the first Abingdon Abbey. It flourished but was destroyed by the Danes when they invaded Wessex in 871. At some time after this Alfred took the Abbey's hundred hides of land into royal ownership, much to the annoyance of the remaining monks, and they remained with the Crown until St. Ethelwold reformed the monastic discipline and rebuilt and expanded the Abbey between 953 and 963. At this time the Abbey owned forty hides of land in addition to the hundred that belonged to the king. Ethelwold secured all these lands for the Abbey and started it on its road to the wealth and power that it exercised throughout the Middle Ages.

This refounding of the Abbey was important for Radley since the area was part of the Abbey lands and its church became in due course a chapel of St. Helen's, which was itself under the jurisdiction of the Abbey. Just when the first church in Radley was built is not known, but it may well have been in Saxon times. The building of local churches had got under way in some places by the eighth century, usually built by wealthier landlords. In due course these churches superseded the old minsters, in which a group of monks and priests used to live and give pastoral care to possibly quite widespread communities. Church parishes also appeared during this period, especially during the ninth and tenth centuries, though the parish system was not fully developed until the twelfth century. While many small churches were built between 1050 and 1100, 'the dominance of the church in English landscape belongs to medieval rather than Saxon times. That familiar feature, the tower, does not really appear till the tenth century' (Godfrey 1974).

As important as the Anglo-Saxon establishment of the basis of ecclesiastical power was the gradual development of the basis of England's layers of civil jurisdiction. The division of the country into shires took place in the eighth century and the Radley area found itself in Berkshire, the name being derived from a Celtic word *bearroc* meaning 'a wood' (according to Asser, King Alfred's biographer, the county got its name 'from the wood of Berroc, where the box tree grows most abundantly'). Subsequently the shires were divided into hundreds, possibly so called because they originally contained a hundred hides. A hide was a unit of land considered to be sufficient to support one free family and its dependants. The actual extent of land varied, however, since a hide was usually 120 acres, though in some areas it was only 48 or 40. There were twenty-two hundreds in Berkshire, our area becoming part of Hormer, which was originally written *hornimere* and meant 'the pool belonging to those who dwell in the horn', referring to the horn shape of the area on the map. Hormer Hundred was made up entirely of lands belonging to Abingdon Abbey, and Marcham Hundred also belonged almost entirely to the Abbey. Both shires and hundreds had courts established and these, among other things, decided problems of land ownership and tenure. Shire courts met twice a year and hundred courts more frequently, but the civil parish did not yet exist.

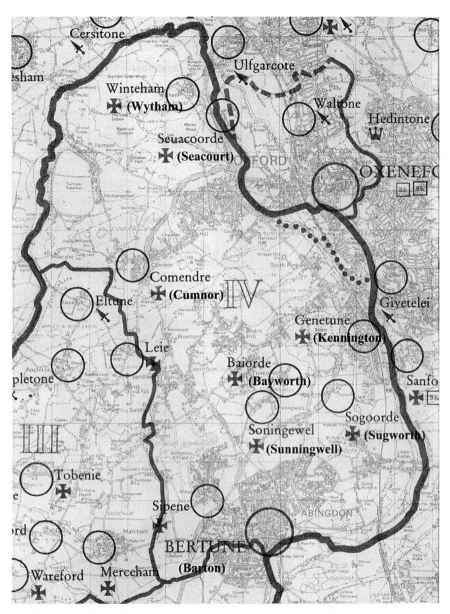

2:2. *The outline of Hormer hundred superimposed on a modern ordnance survey map. The circles indicate settlements at the time of Domesday and the crosses mark ecclessiastical holdings. From* The Berkshire Domesday *(Alecto Historical Editions, London 1988).*

There were also, at a more local level, manorial courts. The manorial system had grown up gradually during the period, possibly as an extension of the villa system of the Romans. It was a way of organizing large estates under one ownership. The lord of the manor would typically keep part of his lands 'in demesne', that is under his own immediate control, and would let out the rest in return for rent or service or a mixture of both. This arrangement, therefore, can be said to have formed the basis for the feudal system that developed under the Normans. Before the Conquest Abingdon Abbey owned 35 manors in several different hundreds and 513.5 hides, bringing in rents of £382. One of the large manors in the area was that of Barton, which included Abingdon and most of Hormer Hundred. Radley, it seems, continued to be part of the manor of Barton until the sixteenth century.

The population of these units was still fairly scattered, though by the eleventh century town-dwellers made up about ten per cent of the whole (Dyer 1994). In Berkshire the area north of the Downs was more populated and more urbanized than the south. No towns were very large, but Wallingford (probably founded by King Alfred) and Wantage, both of which were owned by the King, were larger and more important than Abingdon, despite the rising power of its abbey. Wallingford was referred to as a *burgh,* a word originally meaning a castle and later a fortified town or a town with some municipal organization and 'more generally, any inhabited place larger than a village' (*OED*). The word *burgh* later developed into our modern word 'borough'. Villages also were still small. They could be quite scattered and often included hamlets of just a few dwellings. If, for example, there was already a settlement at Lower Radley, it could have been just such a hamlet. The development of the so-called nucleated village (the village that we know today with its own church, central meeting place, and defined parish boundaries) was a gradual process and did not really show itself until medieval times.

About a third of the rural population in the eleventh century were bordars or cottars (Dyer, p. 243). Both groups were classes of villeins, who held land in return for service due to their lord, typically involving a required amount of labour on his demesne land. Villeins, in fact, were serfs and were tied to the land; if the land was sold the villeins stayed with it. This made them different from the slaves of the Romans and others, who were the personal property of their masters. The difference between bordars and cottars was very slight. A bordar might hold as much as fifteen acres or as little as a house and garden, whereas a cottar, or *kotsetla,* lived in a cottage and might hold a small amount (perhaps five acres, often much less) of arable. Such would have been the status of most residents of Radley in the eleventh century.

Farming in the Saxon period was mostly arable and the main crops in the south of England were wheat, barley, oats, rye and legumes (Clarke, p. 43). Root vegetables appear to have come later. Further afield, in the Vale of White Horse, there were dairy farms, at least three of which in the tenth century produced cheese. Otherwise cattle would have been kept on a local basis, with oxen being the main draught animals. 'The Anglo-Saxon saw worldly wealth as horned and four-legged' (Martin, p. 62). Fields were ploughed by teams of oxen pulling ploughs, and a team might have as many as eight oxen. It is said there were 81,000 teams mentioned in the *Domesday Book.* Some pigs may have been kept domestically, but swine and boar were hunted in the forests, as, of course, were deer. Sheep may already have been grazing on the Berkshire Downs.

There is little mention of pasture in the *Domesday Book,* though there are references to common pasture in both Oxford and Cambridge. There are, however, many listings of meadows, denoting low-lying land liable to flood and used for growing hay, such as the Radley water meadows beside the Thames. There are also references to 'waste', a Norman word meaning uncultivated land, either wilderness or arable that was worked out or had been found to be insufficiently productive.

An important feature of farming during this period was the shift in field patterns, which took place over several centuries. Celtic fields were square or rectangular and enclosed, and the early Saxons probably found it convenient to continue this pattern. With the emergence of large estates (manors) and a more peaceful climate, there was a movement toward larger and more open fields in which different portions would be held by different persons or estates. This led by the ninth century to the gradual introduction of strip farming. Under this system large fields were divided into ridge-and-furrow strips. Some of these were held and cultivated by individual villeins or families, while others were held by demesnes or individual landowners and were cultivated by the villeins and other smallholders as part of their dues of service. It was normal for one individual to hold several strips in various fields. An advantage of the system was, in theory, that good and bad parcels of land were fairly distributed; the disadvantages were that it was wasteful and gave no encouragement for the improvement of the land.

In later centuries, as the feudal system relaxed and broke down, this system led to activities being centred on the nucleated village with its own open field or fields, with pasture in due course being created by fallow rotation (Austin, p.48). Strip farming is known to have continued in Radley till at least the seventeenth century, and one can still see evidence of its ridges and furrows in the ground pattern of some fields. Incidentally, the evolution of strip farming would not have been possible without the introduction of the mouldboard plough, which naturally turned a furrow, as opposed to the smaller straight-bladed hand plough, which merely cut a slit in the surface of the soil.

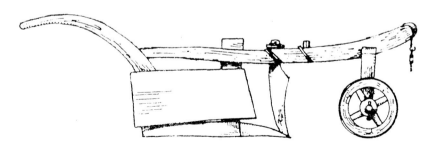

2:3. A mouldboard plough.

At Barton, of which Radley was a part, the large demesne was probably farmed under the control of a monk-reeve, and strip farming undoubtedly helped the farms to supply the food required of them. The 'Abbey relied for its produce principally on the great demesne farm of Barton, which ultimately stretched as far as the high ground overlooking Oxford' (Miles 1986, p. 4). It must be remembered also that this huge estate would have included a variety of soils – gravel, clay and flood-plain – as well as a rich supply of woodland, making it all the more productive of a variety of crops and game.

In 1066 came the Norman invasion and conquest of England, and the question of land ownership took on new importance. References have already been made to the *Domesday Book,* which was compiled in 1067-87. It was ordered by William I and intended to be a comprehensive and definitive listing of land holdings throughout the country. Because the manorial/feudal system depended on fees and services being due from the nobles to the king, from lords of the manor to the nobles (or sometimes directly to the king), and from free tenants and villeins to lords of the manor, so William wanted to know exactly who owned what and how much was due to him and to the nobles. In other words, he wanted to maximize his profits. So it was that the results listed properties not only by area but also by the number of plough-teams, oxen, etc. The eagle eye of bureaucracy had opened in England!

Over time the *Domesday Book* acquired other uses. Throughout the Middle Ages it was the point of reference in the settlement of disputes concerning royal lands, manorial estates, the status of villeins, and other matters relating to property rights. 'Disputes over monastic boroughs such as St. Alban's or Abingdon or over royal rights to tallage (a kind of tax) in towns were resolved in the light of evidence of Domesday Book' (Loyn, p. 21).

The Berkshire section of the *Domesday Book* (headed *Berrochescire* on the title page and spelt *Berchscire* on subsequent pages, which were presumably written later) lists first the lands belonging to the king, then those of several bishops, and then the lands of Abingdon Abbey under various hundreds, Hormer (*Hornimere*) coming first. The first paragraphs state that the Abbey holds Cumnor, which may have been a separate manor ('It has always belonged to the abbey') and specifies several individuals there as being direct tenants of the abbot. It then states (*Domesday* 1988):

2:4. A paragraph from Domesday, *translated below.*

The abbey itself holds Barton *(Bertune)* in demesne. T.R.E. (in the time of King Edward) it was assessed at 60 hides; now at 40 hides. There is land for 40 ploughs. In demesne are 3 ploughs; and 64 villans [villeins] and 36 bordars with 34 ploughs, and 10 merchants dwelling in front of the door of the church paying 40*d.*, and in Abingdon 2 slaves and 24 coliberts [cottars], and 2 mills rendering 40*s.*, and 5 fisheries rendering 18*s.* 4*d.*, and 200 acres of meadow, and 15*s.* from pasture, and 2 mills in the court of the abbot without rent. T.R.E. it was worth £20; and afterwards, as now, £40.

The entry goes on to list several more direct tenants of the abbot, including Reginald, who 'holds of the abbot in pledge' the manor of Shippon, two men with 10 hides in Bayworth, and one man holding 4 hides in Sugworth, another with 5 hides in Sunningwell and Kennington, and yet another with 1 hide in Kennington. There is, alas, no mention of Radley. This does not mean that it did not exist, simply that the abbot had no direct tenants there.

It would be logical, before closing this chapter, to say something about transport and communications during the Saxon period. Sadly, however, there is very little evidence to go on. The Saxons inherited from the Romans a road system that had been developed mainly to serve the needs of the Roman garrisons around the country. This system must have been adapted and expanded to serve the many settlements that sprang up and the gradually developing manors and boroughs. Besides, the military need continued, and armies were surprisingly mobile. In 1066, King Harold took his army from Stamford Bridge on the Humber to Hastings in a fortnight (Martin, p. 64), though they may well have been too tired to fight effectively when they got there. William I, once he had taken charge, travelled widely through the country, and in 1086 he sent his messengers all over the country to gather information for the *Domesday Book*. Presumably they travelled by horseback, but some of their journeys may have been made by river. It is known that heavy goods, such as building stone, were carried by water, and people also used the waterways for travel. Wallingford, for example, 'owed carrying services to the king, either by land with horses or upstream and downstream on the Thames between Benson and Reading' (Martin, p. 62).

At a more local level there would have been roads, or at least tracks, between settlements. The monk-reeve of Barton, for example, would have needed to travel through the Barton estates, and the villeins on the land would have needed to travel to courts, fairs, and markets. These would, on the whole, have been short journeys, not longer than a day's travelling on foot, ass, or horse. It would be interesting to know if there were residents in Lower Radley at this time and whether the old road from Pumney to Thrupp and on to Abingdon already existed. If it did, it would probably have led directly to Abingdon Abbey, where some of the villeins might have had business or menial employment.

To sum up, the beginning of the Anglo-Saxon period was marked by small, often short-lived settlements and a great deal of fighting. For a considerable time our area was fought over between West Saxons and Mercians and was then attacked by the Danes. Despite all this the period saw the beginnings of modern England. Shires, hundreds, and church parishes were established that still remain today. Alfred encouraged learning and gave the country its first system of laws, and, out of several Germanic dialects, a standard language emerged, at least for southern England. At the same time Christianity spread throughout the country, and the beginnings of ecclesiastical power and organization were laid. Finally, twenty years after the Norman invasion, the ownership of land was codified in the *Domesday Book*. It can be emphasized, however, that, while the ownership of the country changed under the Normans, the legal and administrative structures established by the Saxons remained. Nor did the Normans really change the social order; they simply imposed their feudal system on the existing similar but less sophisticated manorial system.

Chapter 3

Medieval Times

The name of Radley first occurs in the late twelfth century when Radley provided wax for the altar of the abbey church, and the tithe from the men of Radley was devoted to the fabric (*VCH, Berks,* IV, pp. 411-2). In the second of these entries Radley is said to be in 'the tenure of Barton', as it was in the Domesday Survey, and it presumably remained so until the Dissolution in 1538. William the Conqueror levied very heavy taxes before leaving for his attempt to seize Normandy, where he eventually died fighting against the French king Philip I. William's successor, William Rufus, was very harsh and hated by all his people. He extorted money from the monasteries whenever he could for his costly campaigns against France, often putting the abbeys in a serious financial position. Henry I, later in his reign, was to treat the Church in much the same way.

Good terms between royalty and the abbot were as much a political liaison as friendship. After the death of an abbot both Saxon and Norman kings were instrumental in the selection of a new one, and all the abbey revenues reverted to the king until a successor was appointed, which always produced gain for the Crown and loss to the abbey.

In 1189 Richard I (Richard Lionheart) was crowned. Born in Oxford and nurtured in Aquitaine, he spent only six months of his life in England and was more interested in the costly Third Crusade than in ruling the country. No doubt some of the knights supplied by the monastery travelled with his forces. Richard sold privileges to help finance this Crusade, and the monks of Abingdon seized the opportunity to buy the right to elect their own abbot. This right was not absolute and the Crown still retained a great deal of influence. The abbots remained political figures to the end. The crusade was also financed by heavy taxes, and the ransom paid after Richard was captured on his way home added to the strains of the country's financial burden. Town and monastery would have had to contribute heavily to both crusade and ransom.

Abbey Manors

Sugworth (commonly known in the 10th and 11th centuries as *Sawceres* or *Borrowsley*) was once a considerable hamlet. Sugworth Manor (now the site of Sugworth Farm) originally belonged to the Benedictine abbey as part of Barton. The term 'manor' conjures up an image of a baronial manor but in the greater Radley area this is incorrect. The manor would have consisted at least in part of tenant holdings. The tenants would have been free or bound (villeins), rank being determined by personal status or the status of their land. The abbot would have received money or labour services from the tenants. A national tendency in the twelfth century for labour services to be commuted to cash rent was reversed after c.1200 when inflation encouraged landlords again to extract labour services in kind. Labour shortages following the Black Death (1348), when Europe's population fell from 80 million to 55 million, enclosures, tenant unrest and rebellions such as the Peasants' Revolt (1381) effectively ended the medieval manorial system, the final blow coming with the Dissolution of the Monasteries in and after 1538 (see below).

At the end of the eleventh century Warin was holding 4 hides at Sugworth from the abbot for the service of half a knight's fee. These 'fractional' fees, i.e. knights supplied by several families who each paid a share of the cost for the use of the abbot, were added to the thirty knights the abbot was supposed to provide in the abbey assessments for the king's service. This was a continuous strain on monastic resources. In the late eleventh and early twelfth centuries knights were the lowest tier of those who held land in return for military service, and the vill (manor estate) was held in this way by military tenants for some time. In the latter part of the twelfth century Moyses was holding 3 hides here, and John de Chereburk and Thomas de Hynton were holding the estate for half a knight's fee at different times in the mid-thirteenth century. In 1316 the abbot seems to have held Sugworth in his own hands, and in 1428 he was returned as holding it for a fourth part of a knight's fee (*VCH, Berks* IV, p. 413).

The only lay people allowed burial in the monks' cemetery were the military knights, who had to leave their arms, gold and charger to the abbot and their silver and palfrey (saddle-horse for everyday riding) to the sacrist. Manors at Kennington, Sunningwell, Garford, Boxford, Cumnor and Frilford had military tenants at various times during the same periods.

In medieval times the abbey with its many estates was the largest business concern in Berkshire. The manor of Barton provided the abbey with carrying services and 3,100 eggs per year in batches of 300 or 500 at set times. Other manors supplied the same number of eggs, which mounted up to the grand total of 5,000 eggs at Easter and other great festivals. Barton and Cumnor were two of the manors which regularly sent hens to the abbey, and the orchards at Barton manor provided apples. Three times per year five loads of straw from Barton and straw and hay from Barton and Culham were delivered to the refectorer 'for the brothers' feet'. While the monks lived and ate relatively well, the cottages of the poor were no better than hovels and their diets were sparse and limited.

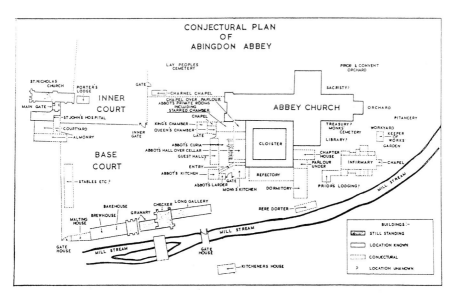

3:1. Conjectural plan of Abingdon Abbey as it may have looked in 1538. Courtesy of The Friends of Abingdon.

The monastery cultivated its lands intensively and agriculture provided the monks with good profits, but the greater part of its wealth came from sheep farming. Berkshire wool did not fetch such high prices as the best English wool, but Abingdon Abbey did very well until the Middle Ages, when clothworkers of Abingdon became more prosperous than the monks. The agents of Flemish and Italian weavers often bought up the wool clips several years in advance. The wool export reached its peak c.1310, but the subsequent decline was partially counteracted by growing demand for English woollen cloth. Throughout the medieval period Radley must have been an active agricultural village, the cultivation of land still being organized under the system of strip farming described in the previous chapter.

Radley Park

After the abundant harvests of the earlier 1240s, the year 1249 was disastrous. Matthew Paris, the chronicler of St Albans Abbey, recorded flooding in the neighbourhood of Abingdon where mills and bridges were carried away, trees uprooted and corn levelled (Cox 1989, pp. 32-3). Radley Park, which covered a much greater area in medieval times than it does today, was far enough away from the river to escape flooding, but it was not safe from dishonest keepers. The park was important to the monks as a supply of wood and venison. The wood was used not only for burning but also for building. Wood and venison were desirable commodities to anyone who dared to risk being caught by the keepers, although they themselves were apparently the worst culprits, for around 1250 the abbot firmly stated what the keeper could and could not do. He was allowed branches blown down by the wind and brushwood, but the oaks were reserved for the abbot. The keepers should not kill any wild beasts. They were allowed to pasture five pigs, five oxen and a horse, but only when the abbot's pigs had had their fill. The main gate could be opened twice a week, in the presence of the abbey bailiff. Obviously cartloads of timber, even a deer or two, had secretly found a way out.

In 1260-62 Henry de Frilford was Abbot of Abingdon Abbey. Rumours soon began to circulate about his granting properties to the keeper of Radley Park (Cox 1989, p. 41). It is hardly surprising that the position of park-keeper was regarded as a valuable appointment. This appears to be possibly one of the earliest records of the monks owning a house in the Park.

The custody of the park was partly settled in 1316 on Alexander le Parker, with the remainder to his son Henry, to whom Abbot John Sutton (1315-22) was said to have granted the service of the park 'in fee to the disadvantage of the house' (*VCH, Berks* IV, p. 411). Presumably Henry acquired land from which the income had previously been used to help support the costs of the property. Henry le Parker and his sons Henry and John are mentioned in 1348. Henry le Parker 'led a great multitude of armed men into evil ways: people going to market were waylaid and trees in Radley Park were felled illegally'(Cox, 1989, p. 54). A Commission was set up to examine serious complaints made by the abbot, which clearly showed prolonged and bitter anti-monastic unrest. No-one was to come armed to the Abingdon markets and fairs. In 1349 animals were killed and maimed. In 1353 Radley Park was invaded by poachers, who took deer, partridges, hares, conies and brushwood. Henry le Parker and his family were implicated in these acts of unrest (Preston Papers, D/EP7/5). William Radley granted the custody of the park to Thomas Golafre and his wife for life in 1371. In 1387, however, the king granted the office to John Middleton with a carucate (a measure of land varying with the nature of the soil, being as much as could be tilled with one plough, with the aid of eight oxen, in a year; a plough-year), a yearly robe and other special profits. The grant was disputed by Thomas Hanney, Thomas Croke and others, all parsons of neighbouring churches to whom William Radley had granted the reversion. The patents were annulled in the next year. Thomas Hanney transferred ownership of his share of the keepership during his lifetime to the Abbot of Abingdon for the maintenance of the fabric (*VCH, Berks* IV, p. 411).

In the Chapel Warden's accounts of 1422/3 mention is made of the purchase of two cartloads of hawthorn bought at Radley Park for fences enclosing two cottages. In the Chaplain's accounts of 1428/9 seven cartloads of fuel bought in the park at 'Radele' with lopping and carriage cost sixteen shillings and twopence. It is probable that Radley Large Wood, which is today classified as 'ancient semi-natural woodland', existed during the medieval period as part of Radley Park.

Bagley Wood

Bagley Wood belonged to the Radley area in the fourteenth century. The Hormer Hundred Court was usually held at Bagley Wood. Earlier students of Oxford found these woods attractive, but so did cruder spirits, for it was recorded in the thirteenth century that many were the deeds of violence committed there, murder included.

In 1327 Abingdon townspeople rioted against the power of the Abbey and attacked the abbey. Abingdon folk carried the sick prior to the Radley woods and threatened him with death if he did not agree to their wishes. By autumn the Abbey was outwardly restored to its old position, but from that time its power and influence were not so great. Twenty-six of the account rolls of the Obedientiars, or heads of departments of the Abbey (the kitchener, gardener, infirmarer, treasurer, etc) are preserved in the Abingdon municipal collection and throw much light on the complex life of the monastery in the fourteenth and fifteenth centuries.

Abbey Fishponds

In 1322 the abbey accounts for the Pittancer, who was responsible for, amongst other things, a fishpond, show 9s.6d was spent on fish for stocking the pond, and in 1369 another entry shows 2s.2d for feeding fish (Cox 1989, p. 55). The nature reserve off the Radley Road, now known as Abbey Fishponds but for a long time referred to as Daisy Bank, was an area modified by the monks for use as fishponds. Parts of the earth-banks are still evident.

The River

The "liberty" of Thrupp and Wick lies to the south of Radley and is bounded on two sides by the River Thames. Thrupp provided cheese for the refectory and eels for the monks' kitchen (*VCH, Berks* IV, p. 414). It is recorded that at Thrupp, a tiny hamlet to the south of what is now Wick Hall, the Thames was in the time of Abbot Ordric (1052-65) diverted from its course to allow the boats of the citizens of Oxford freer passage. It is difficult now to recognize the stream as it was in the sixteenth century. There was then a backwater running from 'Goosey', on the north side of the common called 'Nyett Common', to an island called Pooke or Porter's Eyot and thence to the Abbey Mills. (Porter is a Thrupp family name occurring in the records of sixteenth century wills in the Berkshire Records Office.) This was called Thrupp Water or Nyett Ford. The main stream ran round the south side of Nyett Common. There is no such backwater at the present day (*VCH, Berks* IV, p. 411).

Navigation on the medieval Thames was made difficult by two kinds of man-made obstructions: fish weirs and mill dams. Fish weirs were constructions for catching fish, particularly eels. There were two types. The first was a wooden bridge or frame, from which baskets were lowered into the river. The second type consisted of two lines of posts and wattle hurdles set in the river in a vee shape. At the point a basket was placed in the river in which unsuspecting fish were caught. Both types of fish weir were built out from the bank and were often placed between the bank and a mid-stream island.

Radley Church

The church at Radley burned down in 1290 and had to be replaced at the expense of the abbot. This rebuilt church, built on the site of the earlier one, still exists in parts of the present church of St James. The church restoration in 1902 revealed important information about the building. Among the discoveries was a Norman corbel on the north-east side of the chancel arch, which suggests that some of the original features of the original building were retained in the later one. The architect for the restoration, J. Oldrid Scott, thought the earliest part of the present structure to be the south transept, which he considered to be 'untouched work of the fourteenth century'. One can still see in this transept the remains of the original piscina. Outside, on the south wall of the transept and just below the window, one can see the faint outlines of a medieval mass-dial sundial.

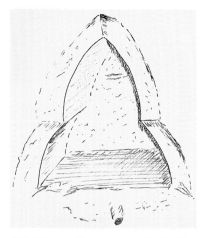

3:2. The medieval piscina in Radley Church.

The consecration cross, now set in the sill of the west window of the aisle but originally placed near the chancel arch, has the inscription *N S M*. It is reasonable to presume that this refers to the bishop who performed the consecration ceremony – *N. Sarum* – in which case it can only mean Nicholas Longspee, who occupied the see of Salisbury (Sarum) from 1292 to1297. Berkshire was at that time in the diocese of Salisbury.

Perhaps the most important find was a great chancel arch of timber, and it was established that there had originally been a series of wooden arches spanning the nave, supported by timber columns on each side. The massive columns and the arcade along the south aisle are thought to be original. The original use of timber columns and arches is said to

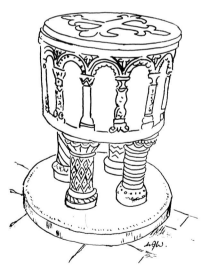

3:3. The Norman font in Radley Church.

have come from a vision that instructed a medieval abbot of Abingdon, when he was planning to rebuild the chapel, to 'seek pillars in the forest' (Drysdale, p. 15).

The fine Norman pillared font dates from the thirteenth century. It consists of a carved circular bowl ornamented with a rich arcade of semicircular arches resting on carved pilasters of various designs with capitals and bases. It was discovered in a farmyard opposite the church, where it had been buried to escape Civil War damage and subsequently put to secular use. It was restored to its present position in 1840. The 'dog Latin' inscription around the base stone tells of this restoration to its original purpose:

VAS SACRUM ANTIQUISSIMUM DIU APUD RUSTICOS IN PAGO NEGLECTUM TANDEM DENUO INTER RES SACRAS SERVANDUM CURAVIT JOHANNES RADCLIFFE HUIUS ECCLESIAE VICARIUS AD MDCCCXL

An English translation is:

John Radcliffe, Vicar of this church, [in] AD 1840 arranged for [this] most ancient sacred vessel, neglected for a long time at a farm in the district, to be at last preserved again amongst the sacred property.

The 1605 chalice and 1571 paten may have come to Radley at a later date.

The original and rebuilt church at Radley was a chapel of St. Helen's in Abingdon and remained so for several more centuries, probably until the early nineteenth. When in 1284 the abbey presented John de Clifford for institution to the vicarage of St. Helen's, the settlement of his income included provision for him to have the oblations and lesser tithes of the chapels of Radley, Drayton, Shippon and Dry Sandford, except for the tithes of lambs, wool and cheese, which the abbot-rector was to have. The document mentions a house with a croft where the chaplain serving Radley was wont to abide. The vicar was to provide a chaplain for Radley and to maintain the books, ornaments and lights in the church (Cox 1989, p.40; Drysdale, pp. 4-5).

It is a widely held belief that Radley chapel was at one time a 'Royal Peculiar', in other words that it was administered directly under the jurisdiction of the Royal family and was exempt from the instructions of the diocese. Legend also suggests that Radley vicarage was used by the monks as a hunting lodge. There is no evidence to support either of these theories or the idea that Henry VII once stayed at the vicarage. On the other hand, why, as Radley was a chapel of St. Helen's, which had the responsibility of providing a chaplain, did it require its own vicarage? Was it indeed called a vicarage in those days? Perhaps after all there is some basis for these intriguing stories.

The Vicarage

3:4. Radley Vicarage.

The pre-Tudor, oak-framed, wattle-and-daub Radley vicarage is said to date from the thirteenth century, although alterations were made during the fifteenth. Like most surviving buildings from this period, it leans to one side, though it is essentially a very stable structure. Inside it is very dark because of the small windows. The ceilings downstairs are low but upstairs, unusually, the ceiling in the master bedroom is high. The entrance doorway, with its four-centred head and foliated spandrels, was one of the fifteenth century improvements. The brick addition was built in 1868 or 1869, during the incumbency of William Wood.

Lower Radley

Lower Radley stands some 175ft above sea level and about quarter of a mile from the river. It is composed of houses dating from the fourteenth to the twentieth century, built on both sides of a lane which runs round a rectangular field 350yds long and 250yds wide. When one of these houses (Grid Reference SU 532 990) was condemned, the owner, Mrs F. B. Levetus, who lived in Lower Radley, very kindly allowed a complete archaeological examination, initiated by the Oxford Archaeological Unit, to take place. The house was a cruck-built thatched dwelling with wattle-and-daub walls, though much of the front had subsequently been rebuilt with brick. The building may originally have been three-bayed with four cruck trusses, a fairly modest dwelling with an open hall, but this had been ceiled over in the 16th century when two fireplaces were put in and stone chimneys built, following a common Elizabethan pattern. The removal of the thatch led to the disturbance of a wasps' nest and displayed the dangerous state of the rafters, which had to be destroyed despite their antiquity, though some of the cottage timbers, notably a fourteenth-century doorway which led to the screened passage, have been preserved and reconstructed in a display at Woodstock museum. Much daub and wattle remained and it made an ideal nest site for several families of mice. Pottery found in the excavations allowed the cruck blades to be reliably dated to the fourteenth century, a date rather earlier than those given to

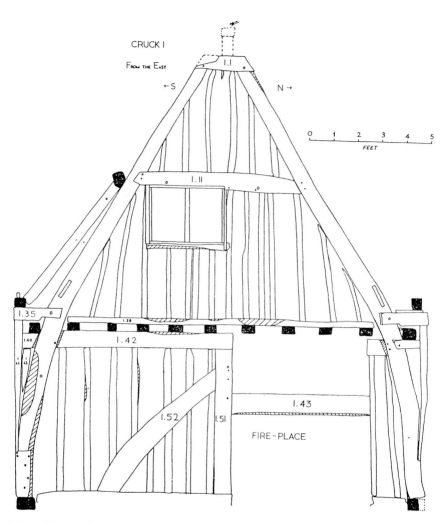

CRUCK I

From the East

← S   N →

1.1

0 1 2 3 4 5
FEET

1.11

1.35

1.38

1.42

1.40

1.43

1.52   1.51

FIRE-PLACE

*3:5. A diagram showing the structure of the cruck house described (**Hinton**, p. 18.).*
Copyright Oxfordshire Architectural and Historical Society.

such buildings in other regions. The sixteenth century daub and wattle, which remained in a few places, used straw rather than hair. It was one of many cruck buildings in the Oxford region, there being another cruck house in Lower Radley itself (No. 46). The nearest well-known example is the Barley Mow Inn at Clifton Hampden (Hinton 1967).

The Dissolution

By the beginning of the sixteenth century Abingdon Abbey, which had been one of the greatest and wealthiest monasteries, had begun to decline in wealth and importance. Increasing isolation from the Continent and the maturing of national identity proved almost as important as matters of religious dogma in bringing the reformation to England. The Pope's lack of co-operation when Henry VIII sought an annulment of his marriage to Catherine of Aragon highlighted the extent to which an alien papacy exerted unwelcome influence on English life. By judiciously forming common cause with Parliament, Henry set about curbing the powers of the clergy and suppressing the cosmopolitan orders of monks and friars. Monastic properties were seized, partitioned and sold off in lots; their privatisation enriched the treasury and created a vested interest in Anglicanism among the property-owning classes. The possessions of Abingdon Abbey, one of the first monasteries to be dissolved, were surrendered to the Crown (Henry VIII) on 9th February 1538.

From the time of the Dissolution, each of the separate manors previously owned by the abbey followed different paths. 'Le Bertun', or Barton Court, had been a guesthouse of the monks. At the time of the Dissolution Barton Manor stretched from 'Pomney' in Radley to Shippon and to Sunningwell, Sugworth and Bayworth. John Audlett had been the lessee of the home farm at Barton, where he occupied a large timber-framed house close to the river, surrounded by barns and a dovecote. Henry VII had appointed him as steward to the last abbot, Thomas Rowland, and Audlett used his position to obtain numerous leases on abbey properties. His wife, Katherine, was the cousin and benefactress of Thomas Reade, who then became the owner of Barton Court (Townsend 1910, p. 124). Reade rebuilt the manor house with stone from the abbey tower.

In 1544, six years after the surrender of the abbey, Sugworth was granted to Richard Snowe of Chicksands. He sold it to John, Lord Williams of Thame, on whose death in 1559 it passed to Margery, one of his daughters and co-heirs, the wife of Henry Norreys. Lord and Lady Norreys sold it in 1587 to John Doyley of Merton College, Oxford, who died in possession six years later. He had four daughters and co-heirs, Margery, Katherine, Anne and Elizabeth, of whom Margery married Sir Edward Harrington, whose father, Sir James Harrington, had married her mother as her second husband. The two-thirds of Sugworth held by the younger sisters were both bought by the Harrington family in 1604 (*VCH, Berks* IV, p. 413).

The Manor of Radley

The site of the manor at Radley was in the possession of William Butler in 1538. The farm was under lease to William Ryppngale of Shipton-on-Cherwell for 39 years from 1519. Apparently the lease did not include the manorial rights for there is an extant Court Roll of 4th April 1537 where the Court is called 'the Court of Rev. Thomas Rowland, Abbott of Abingdon'. These rights must in fact have been held by the manor of Barton. In 1545 the King still held the manor and appointed George Manser as his bailiff and collector.

In 1547 a "grant in fee" (grant in possession) was made to Thomas Seymour (Lord Seymour of Sudeley, Lord High Admiral of England). Thomas was the brother of the late Jane Seymour and therefore uncle to Edward VI, who came to the throne the same year. Thomas's brother Edward Seymour, Duke of Somerset, was Lord Protector for the king, who had come to the throne as a minor. In 1547 Thomas married Catherine Parr, widow of Henry VIII, but she died after bearing his daughter. In 1549 Thomas was executed for treason, for seeking to wed the young Princess Elizabeth, and on his attainder the manor was granted by her brother, Edward VI, to the princess, later to become Queen Elizabeth I, who held it up to her accession (*VCH, Berks* IV, p. 412). Edward VI was always a sickly child and died in 1553, aged 16, of tuberculosis. The suggestion that the Princess Mary once held the estate seems to have no foundation.

In January 1569 the manor was bought, for £938.1s.0d, by George Stonhouse, one of the Clerks of the Green Cloth (who were responsible for arranging royal journeys) to Queen Elizabeth (*VCH, Berks* IV, p. 412). This grant included 'the lordship of the manor of Radley with all rights, members, appurtenances, etc. and all the annual rent of £35.15s.01/2d and services of free and customary tenants in Radley, Northcourt, Thorpe (Thrupp), "Chaundpool" (the location of which is unknown but has been suggested as an extinct hamlet around the site of Chandlings Farm), and Kennyngton as formerly held by the Abbot of Abingdon and the whole site of the manor of Radley now or late in the tenure of or occupation of Richard Butler son of William Butler and all pastures, meadows etc., watercourses, fisheries etc., and all courtleets, view of frankpledge, fairs, tolls etc., and all things pertaining in the field, manor and parish of Radley' (Baker c.1947).

Radley soon became the residence of the Stonhouse family and was to remain so until the eighteenth century. George Stonhouse already had links with the area. His daughter, Mary, was married to Thomas, son of Thomas Reade, the owner of Barton Court, and was to become the mistress and hostess of that house on the death of her mother-in-law, Anne.

The Dissolution of the Monasteries marked the birth of a new class of landowners, who built for themselves houses which were still sub-medieval in style and more modest than the houses of the old feudal lords. George Stonhouse built a manor house after he obtained the Radley estate. A sixteenth-century cottage remains in the grounds of the present Radley College, but it is not known whether this was an estate cottage, a steward's cottage, or the manor house. There is evidence both for and against the assumption that this was George Stonhouse's manor house. Some accounts suggest the original manor house was destroyed when the present Hall was built in 1726-1727. 'The Cottage', as it is still called, is certainly quite a gracious house of c.1570, and no foundations have been found of a larger manor house. The Cottage is of timber-framed construction with lath-and-plaster walls. The basic features centre around a large hall and a screened passage, with a withdrawing room for the ladies upstairs. The screened passage still has the original flagstone floor. There remains an Elizabethan fireplace with the initials JS (possibly either John Stonhouse, c.1602-1632, or John Stonhouse, c.1639-1700) imprinted in the timber lintel above the fireplace (Catchpole & Cardwell 1966).

3:6. 'The Cottage' in Radley Park, now a part of Radley College.

Also on the Radley Park site is a large sixteenth-century timbered barn, which has been repaired and added to and is now used as part of the College buildings. It is known as the 'School' and was re-erected in its present position in 1848.

There is, in the Berkshire Records Office, a voluminous set of depositions regarding an alleged raising of the weir at Abingdon in 1570. George Stonhouse sued William Blacknall, the owner, and Richard Tysdall, the 'farmer' of Abingdon mill, alleging that their mismanagement of the weir was continually flooding and destroying his lands (Thacker, p. 153). In 1576, mention is made of 'Thruppe Locke' (Thacker, p. 138) and, in 1585, of three locks at 'Newnham' kept by John Mollyners.

Since the dissolution of the abbey, Radley Church had remained a chapel of St Helen's and the vicar there was still obliged to provide a chaplain, though the Stonhouse family later took the custom of nominating a curate to fill the post. Radley had the rights of marriage, christening and burial, and many of the inhabitants even in the sixteenth century were of the opinion that Radley was a 'parish of itself'. The Radley Parish Registers date from 1599. Because of this and because a considerable amount is known about the Stonhouses, we are now entering a time when there is more documentation for various aspects of Radley life and more connections with modern times.

3:7. 'Spinney's Cottage', 51 Lower Radley, formerly three dwellings, built before 1600.

Chapter 4

The Seventeenth Century

This muddled century is marked by the uneven fortunes of the Stuart monarchs. Near the middle came the Civil War and the execution of King Charles I, followed by the Protectorate, the Restoration, and later the so-called Glorious Revolution of 1688, while the second half of the century saw no less than three wars against the Dutch. At a more social level the century saw the continuation and establishment of changes that had begun following the Dissolution of the Monasteries and the earlier breakdown of the feudal system. These included the rise of a prosperous middle class and the beginnings of an even newer class that later came to be called the landed gentry.

The settled establishment of the Stonhouses as resident lords of the manor at Radley Park must have made a great difference to the village. George Stonhouse had died in 1573 and was succeeded by his eldest son William, who was High Sheriff of Oxfordshire and was created Baronet of Radley in 1628. In 1614 he purchased the manor of Sugworth, which thereafter followed the descent of the manor of Radley. Sir William is commemorated by the fine marble and alabaster monument, sculpted by Nicholas Stone, on the south side of the sanctuary in Radley Church. The monument commemorates also Sir William's son Sir John Stonhouse, who died in the same year. It carries a lengthy inscription, the opening of which has been translated as follows:

LEARNED READER

Please, whoever you are who has come to this place, know how with unfair foot death knocks at the door for old and young alike and (as you may please) gaze at this effigy. WILLIAM STONHOUSE, baronet, sprung from the ancient and noble lineage of the Stonhouses of Radley . . . .

4:1. The Stonhouse monument in Radley Church.

Whether due to Stonhouse encouragement or to rising rural prosperity, a number of farmhouses were built during the seventeenth century and several cottages were either built or extended. Park Farm (now Park End) and Pumney farmhouse were built, and later Sugworth Farm, as were 57 and 61 Lower Radley (in the late 1600s), Peacock Cottages (82 and 84), and Walnut Cottage, while Bakers Close, Spinney's Cottage, and 46 and 48 Lower Radley were extended, as was the Vicarage, perhaps to house the ever-growing family of the Rev. John Herbert (see below). It is interesting that, apart from Park Farm, Sugworth Farm and the Vicarage, all these dwellings are in Lower Radley. The 'working' part of the village, in other words, with the exception of a few now defunct ancient cottages in Church Road, remained a good kilometre away from church and manor instead of the more usual clustering around the villagers' spiritual and worldly masters.

An important aspect of Lower Radley continued to be its proximity to the river, which provided lush water meadows and gave richness to the soil. It served also as a highway, and there was regular movement by water of people and goods between Oxford and London and places in between. As indicated earlier, there had been difficulties with river transport on the Thames because of the conflicting interests of millers on the one hand, who wished to restrict the flow of water downstream by building weirs and dams, and traders on the other, wishing to transport their merchandise to the most lucrative markets.

'The Thames Commissioners, even though empowered by an Act of Parliament in 1606 to make the river navigable, were so despairing of ever achieving this that in 1611 they actually permitted a load of timber intended for that work to be sold off to Sir Thomas Bodley for his new Library in Oxford. Improvements were finally made, however' (Eddershaw 1995, p. 1). Locks were constructed at Sandford, only a few fields away from Radley village, and at Iffley, and the first barge from London arrived in Oxford (via Radley) in 1635. There is a plaque at Abingdon commemorating in 1649 the construction of the lock there by Sir George Stonhouse, second son of the first baronet. Bulky goods like building stone, malt and other grain could now be moved more easily, perhaps timber too, for it was remarked later (Hearne 1918) that 'abundance of woods have been destroyed hereabouts, particularly a great deal of the fine park of Radley, to which scholars of Oxford used so much to resort'.

While the new farmhouses suggest the rise of the individual farmer, a 1633 Terrier, *A Terar of the common fields, the lammas grounds and meadow belonging to the Mannor of Radly,* shows that the old patterns of field cultivation persisted at least to that date. This Terrier (see next page) lists the fields owned by the Manor and within each field separate furlongs and within each furlong the names of those holding strips or plots of land. Thus at Bowgrave Field (later called Balgrave), bordering on Bowgrove (Sugworth) Lane, Wellspringe furlong comprised some 45 plots. Several of these were held by John Willis and several by Martin Cruch, some others by William Cruch, 15 by The Place, and five by 'Wicke farme'. The Place and Wick Farm, in fact, held numerous plots in different fields, as did members of the Willis, Cruch and other families. Some plots were held by Sir Thomas Reade, although he had his own freehold lands at Barton. In this way we can see how individuals or families could cultivate a considerable acreage within the old system of tenure. A later part of the Terrier lists the lottmeades (the meadows, such as Levery and Stockey, where the plots were drawn by lots at either Lammas or Michaelmas), and another part the copyholders of the Manor, those holding land with a house or cottage at the will of the lord of the Manor and by right of a copy of the manorial court-roll.

The Radley Parish Registers date from 1599, and it is interesting to find in the earliest years family names that are still familiar today. It was in the seventeenth century that the names of the Badcocke (Badcock) families, the Deanes, the Smuen (Smewin) family and the Silvesters first appeared. Anne Badcocke was born to Simon and Jane in 1645, Simon in 1647, Henrie in 1650, Jane in 1652, while Mary was born to John and Mary Smewin in 1678, Ann in 1686, and (as Smuen) John in 1688 and Thomas in 1691. Elizabeth Deane was born in 1628, daughter to Thomas Deane;

A Teraz of the comon filds; the
samae grounds and meadow
belonging to the Mannor of Radly
Note that in the first space is the figure
belonginge to each parcle, in the plott,
In the second space the names, In the
third space thayre requred acres, In the
fourth space the measure of them

1633:

More ffielde

The buttcall parke greate ꝰ shoutinge south and north,
begin west and goe east

		acrs . rodes . pch
1	Tp place or Domarues one halue	0 . 0 . 10
2	forn Willis one halue	0 . 0 . 18
3	Tp place one halue	0 . 0 . 25
4	forn Willis one halue	0 . 0 . 29
5	Tp Place one halue	0 . 0 . 31
6	forn Willis one halue	0 . 0 . 35
7	Tp Place hed halue	0 . 0 . 35
Sum 3½		1 . 0 . 25

The butts all lane endes shoutinge east and west of the
lane begin south and goe north,

1	Tp Place laye one halue	0 . 0 . 32
2	Henery Auexy sur one halue	0 . 0 . 52
3	Tp Place one halue	0 . 0 . 54
4	Henery Auexy sur	0 . 1 . 8
5	Tp Place one halue	0 . 1 . 8
6	Henery Auexy sur one halue	0 . 1 . 7
7	Tp Place one halue	0 . 1 . 5
8	Henery Auexy sur one halue	0 . 1 . 4
9	Tp Place one halue	0 . 1 . 2
10	Henery Auexy sur one halue	0 . 1 . 0
11	Tp Place one halue	0 . 0 . 36
12	forn Willis hed halue	0 . 0 . 34
Sum 6		3 . 0 . 2

Middlegroue hill furlonge shoutinge east and west
begine att Middlegroue hedge and goe next,

1	Henery Auexy sur one halue	0 . 1 . 15
2	forn Willis one halue	0 . 1 . 15
		2 0

4:2. The opening page of the 1633 Terrier.

his son Thomas was born in 1630 and died in 1638; Joan Deane was born in 1635 and her brother John in 1637. In 1606 Elizabeth Silvester married Arthur Haet, and in 1639 Mary Silvester married Walter Crouch, a member of the vast Crouch family.

As for the church itself, we have for the first time a record of actual, named ministers. The church door is roughly carved with the name and date of Rodericus Lloid, 1606; in 'a new hand' the register for 12th March 1612 records from the Bishops' Transcripts the burial of Rodericke Lloyd, minister and preacher, by Rodrick Jones, vicar. The former curate John

4:3. Part of Radley Church door, showing the carved inscription 'Rodericus Lloid 1606'.

Herbert was later appointed vicar and married Joan Averie, daughter of a local family, on April 28th 1628, but her burial is recorded on June 5th of that year. John Herbert may have re-married outside the parish some years later for the next mention of his family is in 1635, recording the baptism of Judith, 'daughter of John and Judith', and there were several other daughters in the next few years. In the burial register for 1667 there is a sad little comment from the modern transcriber, 'Previously a very neat hand starts wandering badly', and on October 13th 1668 the burial of John Herbert, Minister of Radley, is recorded. Between 1669 and 1678 William Carter is mentioned variously as vicar, curate and minister, and between 1683 and 1691 John Stonhouse is recorded as either vicar or minister. Otherwise during the rest of this century and part of the next it seems that the routine business of the parish church was carried on partly by visiting clerics or by chaplains from St. Helen's and partly by churchwardens, as seen in the Burials Register. As for church bells at that time, we know only of a ting-tang bell bearing the inscription 'Henry Wright made me, 1617'. The church plate also includes a chalice, hallmarked London 1605.

It was the church, as far as we know, rather than the manor, that featured in the Civil War, although, as we shall see, the general populace of the village must also have been affected. Indeed the surrounding area was a hotbed of military activity. Oxford had been the refuge and temporary home of Charles I and his Parliament in the summer of 1625 during a 'severe outbreak of plague' in London; seventeen years later the city was again to enjoy the costly privilege of becoming the royal headquarters, only this time Charles and his Parliament were at war with each other. Abingdon, less than two miles to the south of Radley, was for a time headquarters for the dashing and unpredictable Prince Rupert, and later it was the headquarters for the equally charismatic Earl of Essex commanding the parliamentarians.

An incident directly affecting the Radley area occurred on Wednesday, 2nd November 1642. 'All the foote men marched out of Oxford to Abington, and so toward Henly uppon Thames; but in their passage, and within a mile of Abington, there was one Blake, a groome of the Kinges bedchamber, hanged on a tree for treason against the Kinge; he should have betrayed the Kinge and his 2 suns to the earle of Essex at one Sir Robert Fisher's house' (Wood 1891). A further note (ninety years later) states that 'the oak on which he was hanged is still [1732] standing and is called by the name of Blake's Oak'.

It was not unusual in emergencies and in time of war for churches to be occupied by troops, and in 1643 Radley Church, while sheltering an unknown number of royalist soldiers, was attacked by a detachment of parliamentarian soldiers, reputedly from Sunningwell. The parish registers record the burial of two officers and several troopers who were killed in that skirmish, and the panelled altar tomb in the churchyard is said to be of that date (Drysdale, p. 6). Also in 1643, presumably in the same skirmish, it is said that the north aisle and transept of the church were damaged to such an extent that they had to be removed and the open side filled in. They have never been rebuilt and it can even be questioned whether they existed at all, although their foundations were unearthed in the restoration of 1902.

4:4. An altar tomb (the 'Cavaliers' Tomb') in Radley churchyard.

The Civil War brought its full share of distress to villagers and gentry alike in all parts of the country. It used to be assumed that, with any luck and because of bad roads and poor communications, life went on pretty much as usual; but historians now believe that this was not necessarily the case. Armies unfortunately did not march along decent main roads in neat and orderly style like the Roman legions more than a thousand years earlier. Seventeenth-century roads were unmetalled and seldom maintained, and they wound their way through countryside (often unenclosed) of arable, pasture and common land. When the surfaces became churned up or the potholes too deep, travellers as well as soldiers simply found their way round them, often encroaching on neighbouring fields, sometimes destroying crops. The lumbering wagons of army baggage trains, with the all-important artillery dragged by teams of carthorses, tried to use the roads but, unlike the more professional Roman armies, could not march in a long single column and were forced to spread out (often simply to forage for supplies) so that sometimes an advance, or even a retreat, may well have formed a front several miles wide (adapted from Eddershaw, p. 74).

The sight of Radley's sheep and cattle, even if the herds were relatively small, as well as the arable fields, must have gladdened the hearts of the troops with the prospect of meat to be had by whatever means. The Terrier of 1633 tells us that 'Edgemeade contayneth by Measure 16a.2r.20p. on which fedeth in the somer : 34 horses and a half or 69 kyne which is to each horse 77 perches'. It then allots areas of the field to different owners according to the number of beasts held, a horse counting as one beast and a cow as half: 'To the place for 16 horses and a cowe; John Willis for 6 horses; Freeholder for 4 horses and one cowe; Martin Cruch for 3 horsses; Henry Avery Junior for one horse and a cowe; Wick Farm for 3 horsses'. Rather surprisingly, however, few surviving parish records have much to say about this widespread addition to the trials of everyday life in wartime conditions, but claims made to Parliament after the war reveal details of financial hardship suffered by all classes up and down the land, whose often meagre food supplies could be and often were commandeered without payment, as well as crops being trampled and horses and wagons 'requisitioned'. Essex, that aristocratic parliamentarian general, himself deplored the reality that 'being forced when we move to march with the whole army, which can be but slowly . . . the counties must suffer much wrong, and the cries of the poor are infinite' (Eddershaw, p. 74).

There were, of course, other major threats to the population. A look at the Radley burial registers over the whole century suggests reasons other than war for the abnormally high death rate during the months of high summer in 1643. Of the forty-three burials recorded for the whole of that year, there were none at all from January to April and only one in each of the months of May, June, October, November and December. No more than eleven of the twenty-one burials in July were actually of soldiers, including Gylburke and Baines, the two captains mentioned above. The other ten buried in July were all villagers, five men and five women, and are easily verified from entries in the baptism and marriage registers of the parish. Among the names listed, 'John Willis and Mary Willis his wf' [sic] were both buried on July 18th and on 28th Margery Nicholls and Thomas Nicholls Jnr. were buried. This suggests a possible epidemic, particularly as this remarkable increase in the death rate occurred during the hottest, most humid, most plague-friendly weeks of the summer.

Again in August, when twelve burials took place, six were male, six female; this time, too, all those listed appear also in the parish baptism or marriage registers or both. Five burials were recorded in September, including that of John Silvester on 11th September. This figure, although fairly high by comparison with the same month in the rest of the 1600s, does suggest that, if there had been an epidemic, it had passed its peak. It is when comparisons are made with the other decades of the seventeenth century in Radley that the figures are shocking. The registers for each decade from 1599, when the parish records began, until 1699 show an average of fifty-seven deaths in each ten-year period. For the ten years 1640-49 the total was a hundred and twelve, and of these over a third were recorded in 1643, almost all in those eight weeks of July and August.

In today's popular perception of the seventeenth century, the outbreak of bubonic plague in 1665 has become a means of instant identification of a certain period of history, but in fact the country had been 'plagued' by many outbreaks, of varying intensity and in various forms of plague, from the early days of the Tudors and beyond. The Radley burials register for 1643 appears to suggest an outbreak of plague but there were also 'numerous outbreaks of typhus, the occupational disease of armies and the inevitable concomitant of the English Civil War . . . and in many rural parishes . . . throughout the war, typhus caused an exceptional number of deaths. It was quickly communicated to civilian populations whenever towns were placed under siege or troops billeted on villages. The authorities were themselves aware of the need to discriminate between the two diseases. All over western Europe these epidemics were marked [as in Radley in 1643] by a rapid rise in the number of deaths in the summer and burials reached their peak in the months between July and September' (Slack 1985).

It is time now to return to the Stonhouse family. Sir William Stonhouse was briefly succeeded in 1632 by his eldest son, Sir John, who died in the same year and was in turn succeeded by his brother, Sir George, who built the lock at Abingdon and lived until about 1675. He was Sheriff of Berkshire in 1637-8 and M.P. for Abingdon in April-May 1640 and from November 1640 to January 1643-4, when he was disbarred for his royalism and fined the considerable sum of £1,460.

There seems to have been some connection between Sir George, Member, and William Lenthall (1591-1662), Speaker of the Long Parliament, who lived at Besselsleigh and achieved fame in 1642 by repudiating King Charles I, when he came to have five members of the House arrested, with the words 'May it please your Majesty, I have neither eyes to see nor tongue to speak in this place but as the House is pleased to direct me.' It has been thought that Lenthall married one of the Stonhouse daughters, but there is no evidence for this. However, his son, Sir John Lenthall, took as his second wife the widow of Sir John Stonhouse, Sir George's elder brother, who, as noted above, had died in 1632. William Lenthall is said to have protected both the Stonhouse family and the Reades of Barton Court from severe treatment at the hands of Cromwell, and in 1653 he gave to Radley Church the present pulpit canopy, which is believed to have hung over the Speaker's chair at Westminster, the chair

4:5. The pulpit canopy in Radley church.

from which he was removed by order of Cromwell at the end of the Long Parliament (*DNB*). Lenthall, not surprisingly in view of the shortage of reasonable options, supported the Restoration, as undoubtedly did Sir George Stonhouse.

After the Restoration Sir George was M.P. again in 1660 and from 1661-75. In 1670 he obtained a new patent and became first Baronet of Radley of the new creation, at the same time securing the succession to his second son, John, rather than his first son, George, whom he had disinherited, allegedly for marrying without his consent. George, however, was eventually able to claim succession to the first baronetcy, while John succeeded to the second title. There were thus two baronets of Radley, a situation which lasted until the death without issue of another Sir John in 1740.

After Sir George's death in or about 1675 Radley's involvement with the national political scene seems to have ceased for a while, and there is no record of Radley people being involved in the machinations that brought William and Mary to the throne in 1688.

It is possible, though, that Radley was involved in another movement of the century, that of agricultural innovation, and this would certainly have been of interest to the new breed of landowner that had become established since the Dissolution. A work of Konrad Heresbach, originally published in Latin, was translated into English by Barnaby Googe in 1577 under the title *Four Books of Husbandry* and described the cultivation of rapeseed, turnips, buckwheat, flax, hemp, woad and lucerne; it was later reissued by Gervase Markham as *The Whole Art of Husbandry* and was still a respected textbook in 1670 (Thirsk 1967). John Norden's *The Surveyors Dialogue* published in 1607 also continued the theme of a quest for land improvement. 'There is', he said, 'not a place so rude and unlikely but diligence and discretion may convert it to some profitable end' (quoted in Thirsk). This opinion must have been most welcome to the great numbers of new landowners in England after 1538. Norden went on to recommend hops for low-lying, water-absorbent ground, carrots for sandy land, hemp, flax and mustard for neglected bits of land, and fruit trees for hedges.

Radley almost certainly was qualified to attempt two or three of these recommendations. Intriguingly, and as one example nowadays, we find hops growing wild and running riot down Sandford Lane towards the river, again on the eastside ditch between Sugworth Lane and Park Farm, and on the north side of Church Road. Are these perhaps descendants of seventeenth-century plantings?

Of the great seventeenth-century developments in scientific enquiry, epitomized by Robert Boyle, who was working at Oxford from 1656-68, and by Isaac Newton and others involved in the founding of the Royal Society, which was incorporated in 1662, our Radley history can say nothing. Nor does it speak of the huge achievements in literature and the arts. In the next century, however, Radley, through the Stonhouses and later the Bowyers, was again involved in the national picture.

Chapter 5

The Eighteenth Century

Despite the Civil War and the following years of political, religious and social unrest the country was recovering remarkably well by the beginning of the eighteenth century. Political stability had been achieved, overseas trade flourished, and new scientific studies were producing discoveries that would lead to the agricultural and industrial revolutions, which in turn would affect the lives of everyone. In many ways, the Civil War and the Glorious Revolution had left Britain better prepared than the rest of Europe to accept the need for change and eager to lead the way forward into a new age.

Before these changes could develop, improvements had to be made to the national transport system or the new prosperity would have been confined to the major cities. Exciting new imports were arriving from India and America, and the new class of merchant traders was anxious to make them available throughout the country. Roads were in a deplorable state of repair, often little more than tracks which became impassable in winter months. One of the first reforms of the century was that of turnpike tolls as a means of raising money for road repairs. This measure proved to be so unpopular that there were even riots against the tolls, but they were to continue well into the next century. In 1755 the road from Oxford to the south was turnpiked from Friar Bacon's study (at what is now Folly Bridge) to Abingdon via South Hinksey, Boars Hill and Bayworth. It would have been much shorter for residents of Radley and Barton to turn off and take the rough road through Bagley Wood, but that way was known to be frequented by highwaymen. Not until that stretch had

5:1. The toll house on Oxford Road today.

been improved and turnpiked in 1786 did it become the preferred route, and even then it was still considered dangerous; the mail coach was said to have been robbed there as late as 1834. There was a toll house at the corner of Sugworth Lane that still stands and now forms part of a new property recently built on that site. Stagecoaches journeyed regularly from Oxford to London but were strictly controlled by the University. By the 1750s, with road improvements and fewer stops, it became possible to travel to London in one day regardless of the weather. Stage coaches and carriers operated independently from Abingdon with a thriving service to local Berkshire towns and villages.

The Thames had also been neglected as a means of transport. Some repairs had been undertaken in the late seventeenth century, including the construction of some locks, and there followed an increased number of barges carrying coal, timber, stone, chemicals and foodstuffs. However, there were often delays due to weather conditions, especially flooding, when barges were unable to operate for weeks on end. In 1730 an Act was passed to prevent private lock and weir owners charging excessive tolls, and eventually in 1751 the Thames Navigation Company was formed to control the whole river west of Staines. In 1786 a canal linking Oxford with the Coventry canal was proposed but it was not completed until 1790, after the Duke of Marlborough had financed the construction of a further short length of the canal, known as the Duke's Cut, which linked it to the Thames. If Sir George Bowyer, who inherited the Radley estate from his father in 1799, had later been successful with his quest to mine coal at Bayworth (see page 77), there would have been another short canal link from there to the Thames at Sandford.

In Radley at the beginning of the century, the church was still in a poor state of repair and remained without the northern transept and aisle which had been destroyed during the Civil War. Further damage occurred in 1703 when an exceptionally severe storm damaged the roof and caused damage to numerous buildings throughout the district, including St. Helen's Church in Abingdon. There is an inscription on the east side of Radley Church tower which says, 'H. Perrin flattened this roof 1703'. The precise meaning of *flattened* is uncertain; it may mean 'levelled'. Gradual restoration of the church continued, but it was never restored to its original size.

Five new bells were cast by Abel Rudhall of Gloucester and installed in 1754. They bear inscriptions which would have been chosen from a selection offered by that particular foundry and which read as follows:

Treble - Abel Rudall of Gloucester cast me, 1754.
Second - Prosperity to the parish, A.R.1754.
Third - Peace and good neighbourhood, A.R. 1754.
Fourth - When you us ring, we'll sweetly sing, A.R.1754.
Fifth - Hark to our melody, A.R.1754.

During the eighteenth century the church at Radley still remained a chapel of St. Helen's, Abingdon, the vicar of which was responsible for providing a chaplain. This person received a small stipend and was required to travel to Radley to carry out certain essential services each week. However, Radley Church retained rights of marriage, christening and burial, and it seems that these and other duties were often carried out by clerics nominated and compensated by the Stonhouse family and later by the Bowyers. This unique arrangement seems to have been popular with the clerics concerned, some of whom neglected duties in Abingdon in preference to serving Radley. One such person was the Reverend Dr Lemprière, the author of a celebrated classical dictionary, who became Headmaster at Roysse's School in Abingdon in 1792 while already acting as curate at Radley on a generous stipend of £40 p.a. In 1793 he also accepted the readership of St. Nicholas Church at a stipend of £27, but the Sunday duties clashed and he chose to continue with the more financially rewarding sermon at Radley, which eventually led to the closure of St. Nicholas for a short time. Radley already had its own churchwardens by the middle of the 18th century, and before it ended the vestry had appointed a constable, a surveyor of highways and an overseer. To an outsider it would have appeared to be a regular church in its own right. In the village, which by 1801 had a population of 298 people living in 34 different houses, the parish registers showed the names of several families whose descendants are still connected with Radley, names such as Pocock, Weston, Tub and Badcock.

Most of the village dwellings were situated in what is now called Lower Radley, and the occupants would have approached the church by a slightly shorter route before the arrival of the railway line in the nineteenth century changed the line of the road. The park and the manor of Radley with surrounding land had been held, as we have seen, by generations of the Stonhouse family since the sixteenth century, and between 1707 and 1718 the estate was extended with the purchase of the Manors of Northcourt, Bayworth and Sunningwell. As the century progressed, the new prosperity encouraged wealthy and successful landowners to build fine houses on large estates. One of the first in the area was John Churchill who, after a great military victory at the Battle of Ramillies in May 1706, was rewarded with the Dukedom of Marlborough, plus the gift of land at Woodstock and money to build Blenheim Palace. This magnificent residence with its landscaped park was finally completed in 1724.

Sir John Stonhouse, Bart., M.P., Comptroller of the Royal Household, who at that time occupied the seventeenth century manor at Radley Park, must have watched the development of Blenheim with great interest and soon decided to replace his own house at Radley with a new and more fashionable residence. In 1721 he began negotiations with Oxford masons William Townsend and Bartholomew Peisley to build a new house in the park. The arrangements were complicated as Sir John was to deliver to the site the lime, sand, gravel, brick, water and stone. Some stone came from the quarry at Sunningwell until that was exhausted, and the remainder came from Headington. By 1723/24 most of the external work was completed but a serious dispute followed concerning the masons' bills, amounting to the sums of £1226.2s.5d. and £49.2s.5d., which led to a lawsuit and delayed the final completion of the work until 1727. This grand new house at Radley Park, which is now part of Radley College and known as the Mansion, must have caused quite a sensation and is still an

5:2. Radley Hall, now the Mansion House at Radley College, from a watercolour by J.M.W. Turner. Copyright © Tate, London 2002.

impressive sight, especially when seen from the Peachcroft area. J.M.W.Turner made two watercolour sketches of this building in 1789 when he was only 14 years old. Not everyone admired the new house, and Thomas Hearne, the Oxford diarist, wrote: 'On July 1st. walked to Radley or Rodley where Sir John Stonhouse hath built a new brick house, but tis nothing near so pleasant nor snug as the old house'. Even in those days it was hard for many to accept the new styles of architecture, and one wonders what Hearne would have thought of our present day buildings!

A new house was built at Wick Farm in the 1720s or -30s by the Tomkins family, who were maltsters and builders and were responsible for several fine houses in Abingdon, notably Stratton House (1722), the Clock

House (1728) and, somewhat later, Twickenham House (1756). In 1739 the house at Wick was occupied by a Mrs. Elizabeth Tomkins. It was a square building, having four rooms downstairs, five upstairs and a spacious attic, and was built of brick and stone with a tiled hipped roof and a fine wooden shell hood over the front door. This house still stands but was considerably extended in the late nineteenth century. Around 1780 it lost some of its symmetry by having several of its windows bricked up in order to avoid the payment of window tax, an

5:3. Wick Farm house, from a map of 1739.

irritating tax levied irregularly (presumably at the whim of the government) between 1695 and 1851. In addition to the house there were several outbuildings, including a barn and a stable block with a dairy at one end, a brew house and several farm structures, though some of the latter may have been added later. These facilities must have made the farm, like many others of its time, largely self-sufficient. There was a walled garden, presumably for soft fruit and vegetables, the walls being built of stone with a low brick cornice and sloped brick capping. At Michaelmas 1797 Wick Farm was leased by John Tomkins to a John Badcock of Shrivenham, whose descendants continued to farm in Radley until 1982.

In the 1750s a much grander house began to arise on the Radley landscape, across the Thames at Nuneham Courtenay and on a site chosen by the first Lord Harcourt as being suitable for landscaped gardens, which were very much the fashion of the day. Lancelot "Capability" Brown, who had become quite famous for his landscape designs at Blenheim Park, was employed at Nuneham and later at Radley Park, where, between 1770 and 1773, he was paid three amounts of £200 and a final sum of £72. In 1789, when Oxford was already having traffic problems, the large ornamental

5:4. Nuneham House, the riverside, including, on the right, the addition of 1832.

5:5. The Carfax Conduit.

stone structure known as the Conduit (from which central Oxford residents used to collect fresh water pumped from Hinksey) was removed from the centre of Carfax to widen the junction and allow for rebuilding. It was eventually erected in the grounds of Nuneham Park, where it can still be seen from the river at Radley.

Many of the new country landowners began to take an active interest in agriculture and soon realised that land still being farmed in an age-old fashion could be put to better and more profitable use. One notable Berkshire example was Jethro Tull from the nearby Wallingford area, who had studied at St. John's College, Oxford, and had become a lawyer, but his interests soon turned to farming. He realized the need to modernize farming, and as early as 1701 he invented a drill that would enable seeds to be sown in straight rows instead of being scattered by hand (see next page). He went on to devise numerous farming improvements, particularly with regard to ploughing, and his inventions soon attracted the interest of other landowners and local yeomen farmers. Experiments were made in growing new root crops that could feed animals throughout the winter and so prevent the slaughter of livestock each autumn. This in turn led to the breeding of better stock and the benefit of fresh meat throughout the year. The cattle that grazed on river meadows from Radley through to Wytham were said to have yielded milk with a high butterfat content that produced the finest butter in the county. These new methods of agriculture soon increased the value of land and led to changes in the appearance of the smaller farms as they became more efficient. Examples of this can be found in Radley: Pumney farmhouse was extended in the late seventeenth century, followed by Park Farm in the early eighteenth century. Lower Farm and its barn also date from that period, while at 87 Lower Radley a barn, stables and new front block were added to a late sixteenth century farmhouse. At Church Farm the barn (now converted to dwellings) and stables were built later in the century, as was a barn at Peachcroft.

Radley villagers, like many others, were fortunate in being able to grow their own vegetables and often kept chickens and a pig, but their general diet began to improve and become more varied. Sugar was now fairly commonplace with the increasing imports, and the price of tea decreased enough for it to be available to most households by the second half of the century. Clothing too began to improve for the average person, thanks to the import of cotton and the new invention of incredible textile manufacturing machines. The industrial revolution had arrived and developed rapidly; so that more and more people left the country to work

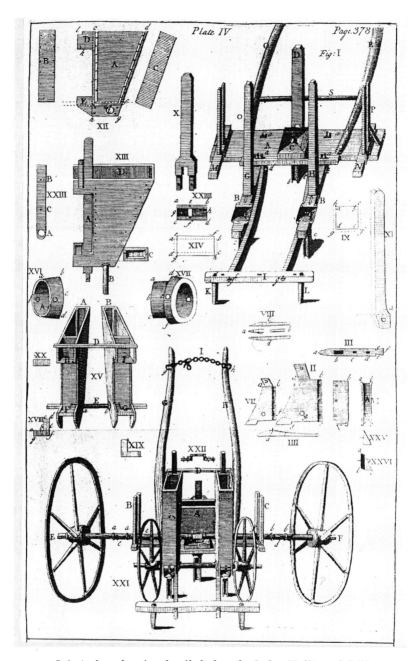

5:6. A plate showing detailed plans for Jethro Tull's seed drill.

in the factories, particularly in the north and midlands. Some cottage industries, such as glove-making and lace-making, often employed people who could carry out work at home. These skills were handed down within families and Radley seems to have been associated with the making of smocks, which were the standard garment of farm workers. This type of work continued well into the nineteenth century.

The Radley connection with the Bowyer family began in 1733 when Anne Stonhouse of Radley Hall was married at Radley Church to Sir William Bowyer, Bart. and moved to Buckinghamshire to become the mistress of Denham Court near Uxbridge. In the same year, not long after the completion of his new mansion in Radley Park, Sir John Stonhouse died at the age of 64, from what was described as a lingering distemper, and he was succeeded in turn by each of his three unmarried sons, then in 1792 by a family niece, Penelope, Lady Rivers, and finally in 1794 by Sir George Bowyer of Denham, a son of the Bowyer/Stonhouse alliance. In that year Sir George had lost a leg in the naval battle at Ushant and had been honoured for his bravery with the award of the Baronetcy of Radley and promotion to Vice Admiral. When he brought his wife to Radley in 1795, they were greeted with great acclaim at Abingdon and escorted to Radley by a troop of local cavalry. The Admiral appears to have been a very popular hero, and he was enthusiastically welcomed. A splendid ball was arranged in his honour at the Guildhall in Abingdon, to which all the local elite were invited. For his bravery, Edward Lloyd's Coffee House in the City of London (now the famous Lloyd's shipping insurance firm) presented the Admiral with a very fine two-foot tall silver vase with unusual nautical ornamentation, known as the Bowyer Vase. In 1870 this was donated to the Borough of Abingdon by the Admiral's grandson and now takes pride of place among the town's fine collection of silver plate. Sadly, Sir George died in 1799, having had little time to enjoy his retirement or leave more of his mark on Radley than a fine avenue of elm trees planted to commemorate Nelson's naval victory at the Battle of the Nile in 1798. Unfortunately none of this splendid avenue from Radley to Kennington remains today. However, Sir George may still be said to have left his stamp, for tales are told of students being awakened at night by the clump, clump, clump of the Admiral's wooden leg as he climbs the staircase at Radley College.

Chapter 6
The Nineteenth Century

During the early part of this century, village life carried on much the same as it had during the previous century under the domain of the Stonhouse/Bowyer families at Radley Hall. It was towards the middle of the 1800s, when the great Victorian era began, that Radley saw new ways of life come into being, brought by education, railways, roads, alternative types of employment and so on. The growth in the parish population rose steadily throughout the whole century. In 1801, as we have seen, it was recorded at 298 persons; by 1811, according to a survey of Radley by a certain Richard Greenaway, it had risen to 337 people living in 42 houses with 66 heads of families. It is also interesting to note that the Census of 1881 included a family of eight who lived in a caravan and were detailed as travelling musicians, so numbers given as population per village included people moving in and out.

In 1849 the total acreage of Radley was given as 2,912 by estimation, of which 1,200 acres were arable, 900 meadow, 490 pasture, 149 wood and the rest roads, railways, waste, water and the sites of buildings. The Tithe Award for that year lists just five landowners whose tithes were merged in their freehold and inheritance, so that they were discharged from paying all tithes except vicarial ones. Of these five, one, owning 73 acres, was Sir John Chandos Reade, Bart., of Barton Court, another, with 258 acres, was the estate of the late John Tomkins, and a third, owning 2,091 acres, was George Bowyer, Esq.(acting, presumably, for his father, who was then living in Italy). What happened between 1849 and 1889 to the difference between these 2,091 acres and the 1,277 acres in the Bowyer sale (see pp. 84-5) is not known.

The Didcot-to-Oxford railway line was opened by the Great Western Railway in 1844, and the Abingdon branch line from Radley was opened for passenger traffic on Monday, 2nd June 1856. The first station at Radley was built at the intersection of the main line and the

6:1. Radley Station in 1873. The Lens Sutton Collection.

branch line near Black Bridge. It consisted only of a wooden transfer platform partly covered by a timber train shed, and it was used simply for changing trains, there being no proper road access available. From the main line the branch line curved sharply away before running in a practically straight stretch to Abingdon. The tightness of this curve was always to limit the line to a short-wheelbase locomotive, which came to be called 'The Bunk'. It was not until 1873, when the branch line from Abingdon was extended three-quarters of a mile north, more towards the village, that the old Junction Station was bodily lifted and carried to Radley and placed immediately south of the present bridge, after which a new station was built on the present site to serve both the Great Western lines and the branch line. This new station resulted in increased commercial traffic, which came in the form of goods such as coal, luggage for the college boys, and farm crops, while the passenger service brought in and took out people from Abingdon and surrounding villages. This is borne out by the report that no less than five trains, carrying 300 passengers, came to a standstill at Radley station during the great blizzard on the 18th January 1881. Obviously not all these passengers were bound for Radley, but the report does give an indication of the extent to which people were using the trains at that period. The first station master, who stayed till 1897, was Charles Ambridge. He lived in a small cottage in Lower Radley with his wife and five children.

With the coming of passenger train traffic to Radley there were inevitable changes in road patterns. Before the line came through the parish the road from the village (Lower Radley) came up from Neat's Home Farm and passed to the right behind the first thatched cottage and in front of the two thatched cottages (which have since burnt down) that stood in the area now known as the Orchard. It then went on up to the church via the top half of Church Road. A level crossing where the road used to be was still *in situ* up until the late 1940s. Another footpath that was lost due to the railway line led from 'Goosey', a pond in Lower Radley, across the fields to Wick Farm, and parts of this path can still be seen. However, one track that was retained led from the village via Pumney Farm, Thrupp Farm, Barton Court and on to Abingdon, a bridge for it being built under the line by the Great Western Railway. This bridge was and still is called 'the Sounding Bridge' because of its echoes. The same track was used originally by the monks from Abingdon Abbey to go to Oxford and in the following centuries by the people of Lower Radley, it being the quickest route to Abingdon.

Still on the subject of pathways, Lord Harcourt, who lived in Nuneham House across the river, had a causeway built from the road in Lower Radley to the river bank in anticipation of building a bridge across the Thames to connect Nuneham House with the railway station. However, the Thames Conservancy wanted only a single span bridge which would allow river traffic through. This was not what Lord Harcourt had in mind as he wanted a multi-span bridge to enhance the prospect from the house. So construction of the bridge was started in 1891 and discontinued in 1892. The causeway, however, is now used by Radley College for access to its boathouses on the river bank.

6:2. An engraving of Lock Cottage and bridge, Nuneham Courtenay, assumed to be the source of the 'Wild Rose' pattern (see next page).

The views enjoyed by Lord Harcourt across the Thames towards Radley were described by Horace Walpole as 'the most beautiful in the world', and to confirm this most potteries from Devon, Staffordshire, and as far afield as Scotland used a scene of the rustic bridge, Lock Cottage and a view towards Nuneham House as a basis for the 'Wild Rose' blue and white pattern in the early 1800s. The same scene was painted by William Turner of Oxford and other artists. Lock Cottage probably served teas, as it did in the early twentieth century, and people could picnic on the island across the bridge. This stretch of water also saw pleasure craft coming downstream from Oxford as well as boats rowing upstream from Abingdon. Of course the river was also used, as it had been for centuries, for ferrying coal to Oxford and for carrying other goods both upstream and downstream.

For the most part life in Radley was quite hard, most villagers working on the farms as labourers or field workers, and in the Census of 1871 there is a record of an eleven-year-old boy being employed as a ploughboy. Women too were employed on the farm as field pickers, but elsewhere there were other occupations for them, such as laundresses, nurses and seamstresses. Two of these, Esther and Hannah Stimpson, worked on a specially commissioned smock for the Great Exhibition in 1851, for which they won a prize (see next page).

Most of the thirty-four cottages in the village were built of wattle and daub between post-and-beam structures and had thatch roofing, having one room upstairs and one downstairs with perhaps an attached side room (usually called a back-house). The cottages in some instances housed quite large families, so space was always at a premium. Heating and cooking facilities were on an open fire or range, and there were no other facilities indoors whatsoever. Every cottage had a well for drawing water and a moderate-sized garden so that vegetables and fruit could be grown and pigs and poultry reared to supplement the meagre wages. The villagers could also go blackberrying, gleaning and wooding on common land during the appropriate seasons.

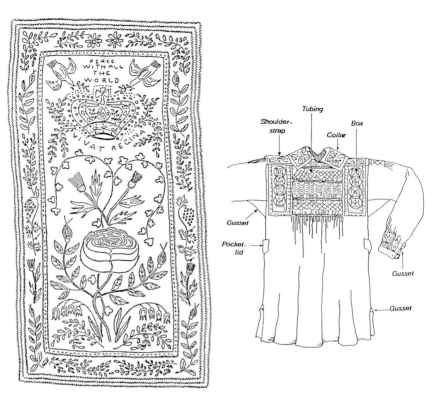

6:3. A detail from the Stimpson smock and a chart showing the different parts of a smock. Drawing by Kathy Sprent. Courtesy Oxfordshire County Museum Service.

Wick Farm, described in the previous chapter, was bought in 1850 by William Dockar, a London businessman, for £12,550.0.0d, plus £577.6.0d for the 'timber and timber-like trees', from the executors of John Tomkins, along with 'two hundred and eighty-one acres, three roods, and four perches of wheat, barley, turnip, and meadow land'. The purchase included a newly built stone lodge at the end of the drive and a labourer's cottage with 4 rooms. The farming tenant at the time was John Badcock, who stayed on and paid a rent of £440.0.0d per annum plus £12.0.0d for the new lodge and cottage. Farm records from 1853 record C.Weston being paid 7s.0d for work at Wick and Thos. Smewing being paid £1.0.0d. In 1863 a receipt from William Bowler of Sunningwell, Brick Maker, records 2 loads of gravel and 400 x 4" drain pipes at a cost of £3.11.0d. An Inventory of Live and Dead Farming Stock at Wick Farm in 1880 lists horses with such names as Trooper, Violet, Dumpling and Prince, with a total of twelve working horses; so this farm must have employed many local villagers. After William Dockar died in 1882, his daughter Josephine Dockar-Drysdale moved to Wick and expanded the house considerably. Some of the farm buildings were removed, and over the next fifteen years extensions were built in two or three stages, including two large reception rooms, several guest rooms and extensive servants' quarters. The house, which had been just a rather smart farm house, became much grander and was renamed Wick Hall.

The Radley Hall estate, having been in the Stonhouse and Bowyer families for 250 years, became financially embarrassed in 1815 over the failure of a quarrying and coal mining venture on the estate at Bayworth. This was the whim of the second Sir George Bowyer, who was encouraged (and perhaps intentionally misled) in 1812/13 by one Sutton Thomas Wood, an engineer and Sir George's surveyor, who was anxious to build lime-kilns for a brick-works at Kennington. Expensive machinery was installed and Sir George began to construct a canal to the river through his park. Some traces of this enterprise are still visible. According to documents in the Preston Papers (Baker, c. 1947), Wood wished to run the business on his own terms, paying only a small rent to Sir George, who had provided large amounts of capital. Finally Wood brought an action against Sir George for unpaid fees amounting to £467.16.8d, in addition to a claim for £1143.9.0d in connection with the brickworks.

These adventures led to the total eclipse of the family fortunes, and the contents of Radley Hall (including 'truly valuable furniture,1600 volumes of books, valuable paintings by the most esteemed masters, and 336 dozen of choice wines') were sold by auction in the week before [the Battle of] Waterloo. Sir George lived on, in retirement abroad, till 1860, and only returned to Radley in his coffin to be buried at dead of night in the family vault (Boyd, pp. 15-16).

Radley Hall and 112 acres of parkland were then leased to Benjamin Kent in 1819 for £290.0.0d per year for a Nonconformist school. When

6:4. The heading of a one-sheet prospectus for Benjamin Kent's school.

this school failed in 1844, the house was rented for a period, but in 1847 William Sewell and Robert Singleton applied for a lease on the house in order to open an Anglican boarding school for boys. On the 17th August their school was officially opened with only two boys on the register and a further boy starting a week later. This was the start of St. Peter's College, later to be known as Radley College, which over the following decades grew and flourished despite the occasional setback (which may have been due to the curse put upon the place by the man who had given it to the monks of Abingdon Abbey, to the effect that dire consequences would follow if it was separated from the Abbey).

The Stonhouse/Bowyer burial vault is on the south wall of the chancel in the churchyard. Within the church are monuments to a succession of Stonhouse and Bowyer family members along with a hatchment and numerous family shields. The heraldic stained glass in the aisles and chancel, bearing reproductions of the coats of arms of Richard II, Henry VI, Henry VII, and Henry VIII (together with a portrait in glass in the tower, believed to be of Henry VII), was given by Sir George Bowyer (Boyd, p. 50) and installed in 1840 by the heraldic artist and glass-stainer Thomas Willement. He may have been responsible for some of the glass himself, or it may all be of a much earlier date. The sidelights in the east window and the centre light of the window west of the pulpit are of continental origin and were given by Dr. Sewell. The carved choir stalls dating from c. 1600, with their misericords depicting cherubic heads came from Cologne and were given to the church in 1847 by Sir George Bowyer. Nine similar choir stalls were also presented to Radley College and the warden, R.C.Singleton, wrote in his diary saying they were 'handsome and good'.

Incumbents at the parish church during the nineteenth century ranged from Thomas Fry in 1801-03 to several wardens of Radley College and to Charles Gore, who in 1893 was the first vicar to be instituted to the benefice. He had already founded, in 1891, a religious order called the Community of the Resurrection, which moved with him to Radley and remained here until the beginning of 1898, when it moved to Mirfield in Yorkshire. When Gore resigned in 1894, there was a delay of two or three months in the appointment of James Nash to succeed him. Although Radley was established as a separate parish, there was still uncertainty over its status. Nash wrote in the parish magazine of February 1895, 'There is, in fact, a difference between the lawyers as to whether there is to be a vicar or a rector, and old documents are being studied.' The decision was that the benefice should be a vicarage, and he was instituted by the bishop to the cure of souls on March 8th and inducted to the church and vicarage by the Vicar of Abingdon on March 26th. During Nash's incumbency, plans were drawn up for a new rood screen and canopy for the east end of the church and also for a spacious and impressive sacristy which would have extended northward from the chancel. However, these plans were too ambitious and were never implemented; but Charles Longland, the vicar who succeeded Nash in 1898, had many repairs and improvements made to the church. The late Norman font, which had lain buried in the farmyard across the road at Church Farm since the Civil War, was found in 1840 and restored to the church. In 1897 the tenor bell in the tower was cast and hung to commemorate the diamond jubilee of Queen Victoria.

The vicarage, which was built in the 13th century, had a red brick addition added to it in 1868/9 during the incumbency of William Wood, though the two buildings were separated some 120 years later.

To the southeast of the church, just outside the churchyard, stood the village smithy and the smithy pond. We know from old maps and pictures that the smithy was still *in situ* as late as 1885, but the pond is all that now remains.

The village school also adjoins the churchyard. The 1870 Education Act brought elementary education within reach of all children, and the red brick section of the school was probably built in 1871, but the school house is a much earlier building. We do have records in the 1851 census showing that some children were described as scholars but others of the same age were not. It may be that some parents could afford to pay for their children's education, but where the schooling took place is not confirmed. In 1871 rough sketches for a school at Radley were sent to the Warden at Radley College for his perusal. One drawing (reproduced on page 83) shows two classrooms with a coal store and ancillary outbuilding to the rear. In 1875 the third Sir George Bowyer leased the land on which the school stood to the vicar and churchwardens for a sum of £1.6.0d per year for a term of 99 years, but in 1897 Mary Bowyer gave all the said land, i.e. one rood and three perches, to the vicar and churchwardens, together with the school building and premises thereon. The school at Radley was from the very beginning a Church of England

6:5. An engraving showing Radley Church with the smithy and its pond in the foreground.

school. The head teacher in 1893, Mary Tyrrell, reported in a letter that when she came to the school the Warden had allowed her to fix her own salary, this being the sum of £5.16.8d per month.

Radley being a farming community would have seen the schoolchildren helping out in the fields at harvest time and with various other tasks around the farms. Also they must have suffered with all the childhood ailments and been away from school for quite long periods, so teaching must have been quite a frustrating task. Prize-giving at the school was held just before Christmas. The prizes consisted of a paper bag containing a bright new penny, an orange and a bun.

Most important village events took place in the school as only about twenty people could be fitted into the Cabin, which was a tiny building in Lower Radley where the Band of Hope met every Wednesday. May Day celebrations, however, were held in The Close, the field in the centre of Lower Radley, with the children dancing around the maypole, and a big tea was held for everyone. The beginning of August was Radley Feast time, with the Bowyer Arms brewing ginger beer especially for the occasion. The fair people with their caravans and side-shows camped on the opposite side of the road to the Bowyer Arms, on what is now New Road. They came on the second Sunday in August and stayed for a week. This feast never survived the first World War. Harvest Home was another occasion for merrymaking, when the last load was brought in with due pomp and ceremony. Guy Fawkes Night appears to have been marked by two large bonfires, one at Neat's Home Farm and another at Lower Farm, with the villagers making the most of both parties. On Christmas Day the village charities for 'poor and industrious' persons were announced from the pulpit, recipients going to church the next day to receive their gifts of bread with three coats for the men and three blankets for the women. Boxing Day saw Mrs. Dockar-Drysdale's brake leaving every cottager with half a pound of tea and a blanket. In earlier times there was also a Hand-Bell and Bellringers' Supper.

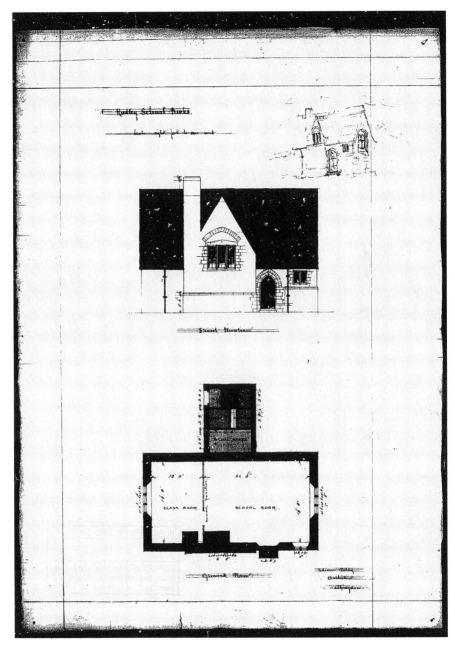

6:6. An architect's drawing for Radley Village School. Berkshire Record Office.

The 'Bowyer Arms', which is the only public house in the village, is situated alongside the railway station. It was built about the middle of the century and was constructed of brick on the site of an earlier farmhouse, with most of the wooden outbuildings being retained for use by the publican for stabling, for housing the carriages and carts and for storage facilities. Morland, the Abingdon brewers, rented the inn and all facilities from the Bowyer estate until it was sold to them in 1889.

During this century the Radley district was, as ever, rich in flora. The snake's head fritillary, in both mauve and white forms, grew abundantly in the water meadows along the river, and the adder's tongue fern also grew in the damp fields. There were many other plants and flowers to be seen in the parish, including moschatel, garlic, chervil, hound's-tongue, creeping jenny, wild hop, mignonette, nettle-leaved campanula and a rare thistle (*Carduus pycnocephalus*). Butterflies and moths too were abundant in their different colours and varieties, and the hay fields, hedges, copses and woods provided a rich source of plant life and flowers for them to feed on.

With the closing years of the nineteenth century the villagers of Radley were still predominantly working on the farms and inhabiting the same cottages as their predecessors had over the past 100 years. There had been advancements made in the form of travel from horse and cart, carriage or wagon to the much speedier train, although for the poorest families travel on foot was still the custom. Their living and working conditions depended a lot on their employers looking after them, and if they were unable to work they were often thrown out of their homes and onto the roads.

In 1889 the Bowyer Estate was put up for sale and so ended the Bowyer connection with Radley. The sale was held at the Auction Mart, Tokenhouse Yard, Lothbury, London on the 2nd July and the major purchaser was Mrs. Dockar-Drysdale of Wick Hall, who (by prior arrangement) immediately disposed of Radley Hall and its 136 acres to the Trustees of Radley College for £13,000. Thus the College at last acquired the freehold to its property.

IN THE HIGH COURT OF JUSTICE.
CHANCERY DIVISION.
MR. JUSTICE KAY.

THE RADLEY HALL ESTATE,
BERKSHIRE.

PARTICULARS
OF A

FREEHOLD PROPERTY,
KNOWN AS THE

RADLEY HALL ESTATE,

Situate in the Parishes of Radley and St. Helen's, Abingdon, adjoining the Radley Station, on the Great Western Railway, about Two Miles from Abingdon, and only Four from the City of Oxford. It comprises a

Mansion known as
RADLEY HALL,

Situate in the centre of a Park, with Pleasure Grounds and Stabling Premises, let on Lease to the Trustees of Radley College; also

The Church, Neat Home, Walsh's and Minchin's Farms,

With Farmhouses, Homesteads, and Arable and Grass Lands, numerous smaller Occupations, Ground Rents secured upon "The Bowyer Arms" and Two Semi-detached Villa Residences;

ALSO

RADLEY GREAT WOOD;

AND

Forty-four Cottages and Gardens, Allotment Gardens, and some Detached Lands,

THE WHOLE CONTAINING ABOUT

1277 Acres and 21 Perches,

And producing (inclusive of the Annual Value of the Woods and Plantations in Hand) the Rental of about

£1828 : 9 : 4 A YEAR.

The River Thames bounds the Property for over Two Miles, on the other side of which are the "Nuneham Woods" belonging to E. W. HARCOURT, Esq.

TO BE SOLD BY AUCTION BY

Mr. ROBERT COLLIER DRIVER,
OF THE FIRM OF

Messrs. DRIVER & CO.,

With the approbation of Mr. Justice Kay, the Judge to whose Court this Cause is attached.
AT THE AUCTION MART, TOKENHOUSE YARD, LOTHBURY, LONDON,

On TUESDAY, the 2nd day of JULY, 1889,

At TWO O'CLOCK precisely, in LOTS, unless an acceptable offer for the whole or any Lot be previously made by Private Treaty.

To be viewed by Orders only to be obtained of Messrs. DRIVER & CO., and with the Permission of the Lessees and Tenants.

Printed Particulars may be obtained at the Crown and Thistle, Abingdon; the Bowyer Arms, Radley; at the Mitre and Clarendon Hotels, Oxford; the Queen's, Reading; at the Auction Mart and Estate Exchange, Tokenhouse Yard, Lothbury; of
Messrs. HULBERTS & HUSSEY, Solicitors, 10 New Square, Lincoln's Inn; of
Messrs. MARKBY & CO., Solicitors, 57 Coleman Street, E.C.; of
Messrs. WARING & NICHOLSON, Surveyors, &c., 55 Parliament Street, S.W.; of
Mr. JOHN WEST, West Saint Helens, Abingdon; and of
Messrs. DRIVER & CO., Surveyors, Land Agents, and Auctioneers, 4 Whitehall, S.W.

6:7. The Bowyer sale, front page of the catalogue.

At the end of the century the population of the village had more or less doubled, probably due to the railway and the college bringing in new employees, although one of the local families had a child almost every year from 1858 until 1879!

So the latter half of the century brought major changes in land ownership to Radley, the first such dramatic changes for 400 years. The landscape itself had altered with the railway splitting the parish in half, and the coming of the trains had wrought changes in the lives of many people. However, Radley remained a farming community and the fields and woods mostly retained their previous boundaries. The footpaths that were lost due to the railway were resited where possible along new road systems. But, with the coming of the new century, Radley was again to experience drastic social and economic change.

6:8. Radley's Victorian letter box,
still in use.

Chapter 7

The Twentieth Century

It may be that more changes have taken place within the village during this century than at any other period. From records and documents available, we can imagine what life was like at the turn of the century – housing, working conditions and life in general in this quiet rural community – but our predecessors could have had no idea as to what would happen in the village during the next hundred years. The village population has quadrupled, commuters travel up to a hundred miles or so every day, and housing and scenery have all changed almost beyond recognition.

Today the parish extends from Sandford Lock in the east, from where the boundary follows the line of the river south and west towards Abingdon. It then takes a route north, skirting the east side of Abingdon and along Audlett Drive and Twelve Acre Drive, crossing the round-about and then going northward to the west of Lodge Hill and Bayworth Manor, after which it follows the Oxford Road almost to Chandlings School, when it turns eastward and follows the edge of Bagley Wood and the north edge of Radley Large Wood, returning via Sandford Lane to the lock, covering a total of approximately 3,700 acres. Several boundary changes were made during the twentieth century, mostly to the west side of the parish and arising from the inclusion and then exclusion of parts of the Peachcroft estate. Such changes are reflected in the population count in 1981 as 3,562 persons and in 1991 as 2,290. Whilst on the subject of population, in the census of 1901 the population was 592, but in 1911 it was 927. However, in this latter year the masters and scholars of St.Peter's College had not left for the Easter vacation as they had in 1901, which accounts for much of the difference. In 1974 Radley, along with the rest of the Vale of White Horse, was taken from Berkshire and put into Oxfordshire. The village still had three levels of local government, now called county, district and parish.

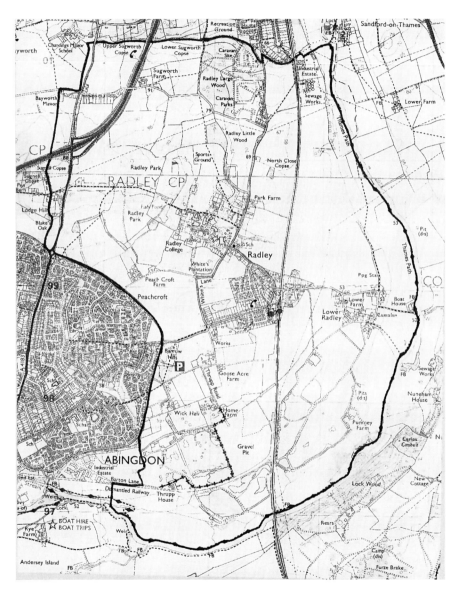

7:1. Radley: present boundaries of the civil parish.

The River Thames, which has always been a natural boundary of the parish, has also been a scene of considerable activity. Throughout the century it has been used by the boys from Radley College for swimming and rowing, pleasure craft from miles up and down the river have passed along it, while fishing has been a popular riverside sport. In

7:2. Radley College boathouses, boatman's cottage on the left, c. 1930.

1943, during the second world war, the Oxford and Cambridge Boat Race was held over a short course of 1¼ miles on Radley's stretch of the river between Sandford Lock and Radley. Oxford won the race, which attracted some 7-10,000 spectators!

In the severe winter of 1947 the river froze across and in the later floods, ensuing from the rapid thaw of snow, most of Lower Radley was completely cut off. The floods were due also to Sandford Lock breaking under the pressure of water flowing downstream. The Rev. J.V.Pixell wrote in the parish magazine that spring, 'We have had the severest winter for years followed by unusually bad floods, shortage of fuel and gales of exceptionally heavy and prolonged character, but we have survived them all'.

The Thames has also been used for centuries for the transportation of cargo upstream to Oxford and as far downstream as London. Even in the 1940s cargo was still carried on barges towed by tugs. Today passenger boats (still called steamers) run from Oxford to Abingdon daily throughout the summer, the picturesque scenery through Radley and Nuneham being admired by all.

The rush beds along the banks of the river have been cut for centuries for different uses and are now cut annually for the restoration of chair seats. A few years ago an order for 500 chair seats to be restored for Salisbury Cathedral was completed with rushes cut from the Radley beds amongst others.

Turning to the land, huge changes have taken place during the century in both the ownership and use of land. In 1900 the largest landowner in the village was Mrs. Josephine Dockar-Drysdale, who had purchased land from the Bowyer estate in 1889 and much of Lower Radley from Lord Harcourt in 1893; at her death in 1921 she owned over 3,000 acres. However, since then a lot of her land has been sold, some to Radley College and some for building and gravel extraction, the remainder being divided among her descendants.

At the beginning of the century there were thirteen farms in the village, namely, Neat's Home Farm, Park Farm, Gooseacre, Sugworth, Peachcroft, Church Farm, Home Farm, Barton Farm, Barton Court Farm, Thrupp, Pumney, Chandlings Farm and Lower Farm. Basically all these small farms were self-sufficient. Each would have had a small dairy herd, a few sheep, pigs and chickens, and on the land side half the acreage would have been given to grass and the rest to crops. During the second world war farmers were asked to produce more food and to grow certain crops such as sugar beet and potatoes. With machinery and chemicals being introduced much more could be achieved. Farmers started to specialize, and the small hedged farms gradually began to merge and make way for the large open spaces that were needed for modern machinery, so that by the 1970s only two farm enterprises remained in Radley, based on Lower Farm and Peachcroft. Whereas earlier in the century wheat and oats featured as the main crops grown by the farmers, the introduction of oilseed rape (gold) and experiments with linseed (blue) have brought about colourful changes to the local fields. All through the history of this area it has been recorded how the local population used the upper meadows for feeding their cattle in the winter and the lower area by the Thames for their summer pastures, and this practice was still being carried on up until the mid 1950s by Mr.Sylvester at Sugworth Farm who, with the help of local boys (being paid 2/6d for their trouble), moved his cattle from Sugworth Lane down past the College, along Whites Lane, down Thrupp Lane and under the Sounding Bridge at the railway line to Black Bridge field by the river in April and then back again in September for the winter months.

Before we leave the subject of farms and the changing countryside, the largest change in the landscape occurred when all the elm trees were destroyed by Dutch elm disease, which swept through the village in the early 1960s. This had the effect of removing all the lofty elms from our hedgerows, copses and field boundaries, leaving the landscape a much more empty space. Another natural catastrophe that occurred to mar the landscape of the village was the hurricane of 1986 although, while quite a few mature trees were lost, we did not suffer as badly as many did. However, many replanting schemes have since been carried out by the Parish Council, Radley College and several farmers and land-owners. Some 10,000 trees have now been planted throughout the parish.

There have been, in addition to the changes in farming practices, considerable reductions in the available acreage. Especially since the 1930s land has been taken out of farming for house-building as well as for gravel extraction and tree-planting, while in any one year up to 25% of arable land can now be left idle and designated as set-aside.

As early as the nineteenth century the rich seam of gravel in the area started to be excavated. In the earlier part of this century small gravel pits were dug in several places, including the garden of the cottage at 90 Lower Radley (now Lower Farm Cottage), in order to provide material for the local roads and tracks. It wasn't until the 1940s that gravel extraction by Messrs. Amey, Tuckwell and Curtis began on a more commercial basis, and a large section of Lower Radley between the railway line and the river was given over to this end, as was another large section to the west of the railway line. A new bridge had to be built over the railway in the 1980s owing to the constant succession of lorries, which had made the old one quite unsafe. Some of these gravel pits have been filled in over the last fifteen years with fly ash pumped underground from Didcot Power Station, and it is hoped that in the near future they will be landscaped and restored to agricultural use or parkland. Meanwhile the filling of other pits continues.

As fewer labourers were needed on the farms, the people of Radley had to look elsewhere for alternative work. At the beginning of the century Radley Station employed local men as platelayers, etc. and also

7:3. Radley Station today.

as station staff. Freight such as coal was being brought in and sugar beet grown on local farms was taken out. Radley College boys also used the passenger service of the railway at the beginning and end of term, the local carrier with his horse and wagon carrying their trunks and boxes to and from the college.   Later, another regular user of the line was the M.G. car factory in Abingdon, the transporter wagons being a familiar sight as they took the cars to the docks for export. In the 1960s many branch lines were closed under the regime of Dr. Beeching, and the Abingdon Branch was closed to passenger traffic on 8th September 1963. Radley station's buildings were demolished soon afterwards, and it has since been an unmanned halt. Three special trains were run on the 30th June 1984 to mark the official closing of this branch line to Abingdon.

Lower Radley, which lies within the flood-plain of the Thames, has seen little new development in recent years and most of the older buildings are to be found in this part of the village. If we take a look at the 1761 tithe map of the village, we see that many of the fifteenth-century thatched cottages situated around the central round field called The Close are still there, and some of these cottages still retain their old names: e.g. the Peacock Tree, Dawson's Cottage, Spinney's Cottage. These old cottages, which at one time housed the farming community, have in recent times been purchased by professional people and considerably expanded and modernized. Unfortunately, few of the original thatched cottages remain thatched today, most having been re-roofed with tiles in recent years, and one or two ultra-modern buildings have been allowed to be built. In this part of the village we also have the village pond (which up until the 1950s had ducks upon it but is now filled in), and the old village green, which is situated in front of 87 Lower Radley, has recently been cleared with a view to replanting and restoring the area. This property was originally a farmhouse but was turned into three cottages for farm labourers, and now in turn it has been made back into a single dwelling. The village green was used on many occasions. Rogation Sunday evening service was always held there up until the 1950s, and during the 1939-1945 war a caravan was situated there for the Church Army Sisters to hold open-air services. It is hoped that Lower Radley will soon be designated a Conservation Area.

With the growing population new housing accommodation, mostly in the upper village, started to be built. In the 1930s, Sugworth Crescent and Lane, Whites Lane and Foxborough Road were developed, followed by Stonhouse Crescent in the 1940s and the St. James development in 1962. Mains water and electricity were brought to the village in the 1940s, replacing the wells and lamps that had been used by the villagers up until then. Mains sewerage, street lighting and the first televisions appeared in the 1950s in time for the coronation of Queen Elizabeth II.

7:4. The new village hall.

In 1977 the new village hall was built on the former site of the Radley College vegetable gardens, off Foxborough Road, and the old village hall, which was in Lower Radley (just over the railway bridge) and had been built in 1924/25, was eventually demolished and the site sold for private housing. A sports pavilion was built recently and opened in 1999

7:5. The sports pavilion.

for use with the sports field adjacent to the new village hall. Building in Radley carried on steadily during the 1980s and 90s with areas such as Gooseacre, Badgers Copse (which was the site of the Radley College laundry until fifteen years before, when it was moved back up to the college), Turners Close, Norfolk Cottages and Drysdale Close, which was built on the site of an original steam bakery and later industrial units which lasted up until the 1990s. Since Radley is in the Green Belt, opportunities for further building are limited and, for the present at least, restricted to filling in the few gaps that remain.

In addition to the permanent housing, there are four established sites for mobile homes in Radley. Pebble Hill and Woodlands are Council sites, the land being purchased by Abingdon Rural District Council in 1962. They are now run by the Vale of White Horse District Council. In September 1940, when the bombing of London began, many London people were evacuated to the Abingdon area. A few families who would not be separated were billeted at Big Wood Camp, a boys' holiday camp which was operating during the summers in Radley Large Wood. These families were joined by others and, for the rest of the war, the camp, consisting entirely of wooden huts with central kitchen, dining room and washing/toilet facilities, was all occupied by evacuees.

After the war the site became a family holiday camp and remained so until it became the Pebble Hill mobile-home site. Woodlands also began as a private operation during or shortly before the war. Big Wood Park, in Sugworth Lane, is a private site, opened in 1963. These three mobile home parks are all in what was once the hundred acres of Radley Large Wood, fifty-five acres of which still remain as semi-natural ancient woodland. The fourth park is situated in Lower Radley, just over the railway bridge, and is on the site of a former woodworking factory which was closed in the early 1950s.

People from Radley served in both the world wars of the twentieth century although, since the parish was a farming community, not many men were called up. However, when the soldiers returned home from the first world war they brought with them the flu virus which had been prevalent on the Continent, and as a result local people caught it and unfortunately died. The 1939-45 war saw men serving their country again but in different ways from the earlier conflict. This time men, besides being called up to fight, served with the local Home Guard, manning anti-aircraft gun emplacements in the village and also a searchlight station which was situated on the Oxford side of Park Farm cottages. Another casualty of the war affecting the parish was a Wellington bomber aircraft which came down in 1942 on the fields of Peachcroft Farm and then skidded across the main road to Abingdon, blocking the traffic from both ways. There was only one report of a bomb being dropped in the area, namely in the field by Black Bridge. This was later found unexploded by two local boys who took it to the nearest farmhouse, much to the consternation of the farmer.

As with most villages, Radley fared quite well for local shops and delivery services. At the turn of the century bread was being baked and delivered to householders by horse and cart (bearing in mind that the village at that time consisted mainly of Lower Radley) from 'The Bakery', now called Bakers Close, where villagers could get their large joints of meat cooked at week-ends and on special occasions; and milk came by pony and trap from Pumney Farm. In the early part of the century there was a post office, situated at different times opposite the village church, at Baker's Close, and at 25 Lower Radley. It was eventually moved to Church Road, where it has been since the 1930s. The village also had a grocery store, a garden nursery in Church Road, fruit and vegetable deliveries and a fishmonger, Mr Nutley, who delivered fresh fish every Thursday. Other services came in the form of a knife/scissor grinder on his bicycle and a fish-and-chip van which called every Saturday evening and parked by the Bowyer Arms public house. A general carrier, Mr Slater, came to the village bringing paraffin, candles, matches, soap, brushes, etc., which was exciting to the children because of the smell and the amount of different goods that he carried.

There have also been quite a few small businesses within the village: Shaw's woodworking factory in Lower Radley and the Oxonia Bakery, Heathrod Ardwyn Plastics Factory and Microfilm House, all situated in Thrupp Lane. However, most of these businesses have now disappeared, and so we find that, in keeping with the times, our villagers commute daily to Abingdon, Oxford, Reading and even London to earn their living; they also travel world-wide. At present Radley has a newsagent/village store, a post office and a public house. In 1999 Ballard's, a speciality car sales business, relocated from Abingdon to a converted barn at Park Farm. Gravel extraction by Tuckwells and J. Curtis and Sons is still being carried on in fields near to the Thames. In the last ten to twenty years several commercial units have appeared, namely at Home Farm Barn, which has five units, Sugworth Farm Barns and a small industrial site at Curtis Gravel Pits, where eight business units are located. There is also a small industrial estate beyond the railway line on Sandford Lane.

As mentioned in the previous chapter, Morlands, the Abingdon Brewery, bought the village pub, 'The Bowyer Arms', in 1889, having previously leased it from the Bowyer Estate for £10.10.0d per year. At the turn of the century we can see from the parish census that a Mr. Jethro Sylvester was the licensed victualler there. In his memoirs Amos

7:6. The Bowyer Arms in 1985.

Bannister, who came to live in the village on 31st December 1900 and worked at The Bakery as the manager, recalls that on the morning of the 28th June 1914 'Mr Sylvester from the Bowyer Arms sent his grey horse and carriage and we were driven into Abingdon to be married at the Registry Office there', so it seems that Mr. Sylvester ran a carriage service, just as one of his successors as publican, Mr. Walter Long, did by car in the 1950/60s. As with most villages, the public house has always been associated with wedding parties and funeral wakes, even up to the present day. Most of the sporting clubs and associations in the village hold their meetings there, and it is also here that the 'Good Friday Walk' was first conceived over a pint of beer. The founders, Mr George Steptoe and Mr Jack Parsons, established this challenge on a walk to Oxford and back, and this has developed into an annual charitable event held on Good Friday. A game called 'Aunt Sally', peculiar to Berkshire and Oxfordshire, is also played at the pub.

Radley College, a public school for boys aged between 13-18 years, now has some 600 pupils and is a self-contained community within the

7:7. Aerial view of Radley College with parts of the village in the background. Photo: Dell Davison.

parish. Throughout the century it has flourished and grown considerably. A new laboratory building (which was quite a milestone in its time) was opened in 1937 as well as, more recently, further laboratories and a well-equipped art department and a fine music building with its own concert hall. The college has also built an indoor swimming pool and has developed a golf course, both of these facilities being available for use by the local public. Extensive improvements, including the expansion of housing for both boys and staff, together with up-to-date educational, sporting, musical and artistic facilities, have been carried out in recent years, and 'College' is now rated as one of the top public schools in the country. 'Queens Court', a circular classroom building, was officially opened by Her Majesty Queen Elizabeth II on the 27th November 1997. Many local people have found employment at the school, working, for example, in the kitchens and laundry, in the various offices or on the extensive grounds.

Radley Church has undergone considerable restoration during the century. The Rev. C.B. Longland, who was vicar from 1898 to 1916, was instrumental in organising a major programme of improvements. In 1900 an ambitious appeal was launched, following a detailed report from a London architect, J. Oldrid Scott, on the condition of the fabric of the church. The report noted that the church had been completely overhauled some 60 years ago, but the work had not been entirely satisfactory. Hence the repair work involved much dismantling and rebuilding, and the church was closed for repairs from 14th April 1902 to Saturday 8th November 1902, when it reopened with a special service in which the sermon was given by the Bishop of Oxford. A feature of the rebuilding was the insertion of four new oak arches spanning the nave, which were presented by Mrs. Josephine Dockar-Drysdale as a memorial to her father. Also in 1900 an appeal was made for £200 for a new organ, as specified by Mr.Fisher of Oxford, in memory of Dr.Edwin George Monk, who died at Radley on the 3rd January that year. The money was raised and the new organ was dedicated on Friday 3rd July.

7.8. Radley Church restoration, 1902.

A new reredos was installed in 1910, presented in memory of Arthur Malim, a former chaplain of the church. It was designed in Gothic style by the Wareham Guild and has a carved canopy and arches superimposed over three sculpted and painted panels, of which the centre shows a child Christ in Glory, the north St James the Great, and the south St Frideswide, the patron saint of Oxford.

7:9. Radley Church, the reredos.

On the north wall of the nave is a lozenge-shaped memorial painting with a coat of arms and the motto 'requiem eternam'. Below this a brass tablet is inscribed: 'To the glory of god and in perpetual memory of all from Radley who served in the Great War of 1914-18 particularly of those who gave their lives'. Eight names are given, followed by a further six names under the heading 'And 1939-45'. The introductory wording caused some distress to the Chancellor of the Diocese, who wrote on the 18th December 1920, 'I cannot grant a

Citation because the inscription includes a Memorial to living persons which is not permissible in my opinion inside a Church. The work ought not to have been ordered'. It is hoped that those responsible were forgiven, for the thing was done and their mark of faith and remembrance remains.

The tower screen, in front of the vestry at the west end, was erected between 1925 and 1927, and the gallery above was built in 1963, in which year the church was last re-roofed. Beneath the gallery there is an embroidered picture of Radley Village, worked by members of the Women's Institute in 1971.

The church has seen a succession of other improvements: gas was installed in 1926, electricity in 1936-37 and central heating in 1952. The bells were rehung in 1928 and 1952 and again in the 1970s. A 1962 proposal to rebuild the north aisle was never implemented. Although the interior of the church has seen a great many changes, the exterior has remained largely the same. The graveyard surrounding the church has inevitably filled up over the years, and in the early 1930s a new cemetery was consecrated across the road and some way from the church. When this too became full in 1996, another site nearer to the church was consecrated as a second cemetery.

The vicarage, as noted in Chapter 3, is a fine timber-framed building said to date from the late 13th century, though alterations, as with the church, were made during the 15th century. The oak doorway, with its four-centred head and foliated spandrels, belongs to this later date. The interior with its oak beams and low ceilings still has a medieval atmosphere. In 1868 or 1869 a sizeable brick addition was joined on to the original building. However, in the 1980s the two structures were separated, the brick part being purchased by Radley College and the original vicarage remaining with the church.

In 1983 a spacious and well-equipped Church Room was completed. This is a separate building, lying between the church and the vicarage, which was built by public subscription and partly volunteer labour.

Also in 1983 the organist and choir master at the church, Mr David Beckett, read an article regarding a position called 'The Clerk of the

Green Cloth', which had been occupied under Elizabeth 1st by George Stonhouse, the purchaser in 1569 of Radley Hall. Mr Beckett thought that perhaps this title could be put to good use in the parish to raise funds for charitable purposes. He obtained permission from the Royal Household to revive the title, and now the holder, who is elected by the parishioners every two years, duly raises funds for numerous projects connected with the church and the village. In July 1999 the Reverend Sir Michael Stonhouse, a direct descendant of the family, came to England from Canada for a holiday and preached in Radley Church.

The village school is still a Church of England school and is controlled by a Board of Governors, of which the vicar is one. The school formerly consisted of a large room divided by a wooden sliding door to make two classrooms. One classroom had an open fireplace and the other a large coke stove for heating, which was fine if you were lucky enough to sit close to it but the farther corners of the classrooms still remained bitterly cold in winter. The toilets were behind the school and consisted of three cubicles for the girls (one specifically for the teachers), and the boys' side fared little better. There were no heating facilities so no one lingered longer than necessary! In the early 1950s a further classroom was added and gradual improvements have been made with extra classrooms, a dining room, kitchen and playground, all with up-to-date facilities. In September 1998 a Pre-School for children of below school age was started at the village school, whereas previously such classes had been held in the village hall. There is no state secondary school in Radley, so after the age of eleven the children have to travel to Abingdon to continue their education.

Between the church and the school is the school house, which is owned by the church. In former days the head teacher used to reside there, but in recent years it has been let to various tenants.

Quite a few archaeological investigations were carried out in the parish during this century, especially at Barton Farm, Barrow Hills and the nearby Abbey Fishponds. Most of the digs were examples of 'rescue archaeology', the investigations taking place within a prescribed allotment of time prior to the building of houses. This was especially true of the extensive excavations carried out by the Oxford Archaeological Unit at Barrow Hills in 1983-85, before the development of the Eason Drive and Chestnuts areas. The findings of these and other excavations, which have helped considerably to awaken interest in the history of the village, are described in detail in Chapters 1 and 2 of this book. Further excavations have revealed a late Bronze Age village built on stilts on the site adjacent to the railway line at the former junction with the Abingdon Branch line. Also, again as noted in Chapter 1, with the building of the Abingdon bypass (the A34), a site near the top of Sugworth Lane has been designated a Site of Special Scientific Interest as a result of deposits of pollen from ancient pine trees being found in the making of this road.

More informal searches for artefacts are now carried out with metal detectors. In October 1997 a silver hawking ring ('a varvel'), dating from about 1650, was found in a field by Peachcroft Farm. The outside was engraved 'Radley in Com.Berks of', 'Com.' being short for the Latin word for county. The ring is believed to have been one of a pair.

In 1999 the Radley History Club did a parish survey of flora and fauna. They discovered that the snakeshead *(Fritillaria meleagris)*, which had flourished in the water meadows alongside the Thames during the last century, had, due to intensive farming methods, died out in the 1960s. There remained but two common spotted orchids *(Dactylortiza fuchsii)* at a site where 50 years earlier they had been prevalent. Other wild flowers such as cowslips *(Primula veris)*, violets *(Viola canina* and *odorata)*, ragged robin *(Lychnis floscuculi)* and many others can still be seen about the parish. In Radley Large Wood the ground is carpeted first by primroses, then by white wood anemones, and finally by bluebells before the trees clothe themselves in leaf for another year.

The Radley Oak is still standing in the grounds of Radley College; its girth has now been established at 28 feet. Various methods have been tried to establish the age of this great tree, but they have so far proved inconclusive.

Foxes, badgers and weasels amongst many other animals are still to be seen. Muntjac deer spread widely in the latter half of the twentieth century and are now a familiar sight in gardens as well as fields and woods. Roe deer, which were introduced into Dorset from Scotland in 1800, have also spread into this area.

There are numerous village organisations in Radley. The Men's Football Club, which we know has been in existence since the early part of the century (and maybe earlier), won cups and shields in the 1911/12 season. The Cricket Club was also formed in the early part of the century. The Radley Women's Institute, founded in 1925, celebrated its 75th anniversary in 2000. There are also Brownies, Guides, Cubs, Men's and Women's Fellowship, Bingo, Social Club, Swimming Club, and there is an active Boys' Football Club. The Retirement Group, previously called The Darby and Joan Club, which lapsed, was reformed in 1990 and is now a very successful club having speakers, outings and holidays, its membership totalling 135. The History Club, which started in the spring of 1997, produced a village map for the Millennium in 2000, and its members have now gone on to research the village history and produce this book.

Looking back now over the twentieth century, Radley has experienced all the changes imaginable and, as the Rev. J.V. Pixell remarked, 'we have survived them all'. Housing, employment, social and economic changes have all left their mark on the population and landscape and, as we now go forward into the third millennium, we, in our turn, can scarcely imagine what life will be like for our successors in the next century.

Bibliography

Ainslie, R. (1987), 'A timber-framed house and Bronze Age barrow at 82-4 Lower Radley, Oxon.', *Council for British Archaeology, Group 9 Newsletter 17*, pp. 76-77.

Ainslie, R. (1992), 'Excavations at Thrupp near Radley, Oxon.', *South Midlands Archaeology* 22, pp. 63-66.

Ainslie, R. (1993), 'Tuckwell's Pit, Thrupp Lane, Radley, Oxon.', *South Midlands Archaeology*, 23, p. 85.

Allen, G.W.G. (1984), 'Discovery from the Air', ed. J.S.P. Bradford, *Aerial Archaeology*, Vol. 10, p. 20. Aerial Archaeology Publications, Dereham, Norfolk.

Allso, Sydney E., *Radley Church and Parish*. Abingdon: Abbey Press.

Atkinson, R.J.C. (1952-3), 'The Romano-British Inhumation Cemetery', *Oxoniensia* 12-13, pp. 32-34.

Austin, David (1987), 'The Archaeology of the Domesday Vill', in *Domesday* (1987), pp. 48-55.

Avery, M. (1982), 'Settlement Patterns in the Oxford Region: excavations at the Abingdon causewayed enclosure and other sites', *Council for British Archaeology, Research Report No. 44*, ed. H.J. Case & A.W.R. Whittle.

Avery, Michael, & David Brown (1972), 'Saxon Features at Abingdon', *Oxoniensia*, 37, pp. 66-81.

Baker, Agnes (c.1947), 'Notes taken from Mr. A.E. Preston's Papers'. Radley College archives; unpublished.

Barclay, A., & C. Halpin (1999), *Excavations at Barrow Hills, Radley*, Vol.1, *The Neolithic and Bronze Age Monument Complex*. Oxford: Oxford Archaeological Unit, Thames Valley Landscapes, Vol. 11.

Beckinsale, Robert & Monica (1980), *The English Heartland*. London: Duckworth.

Berkshire Archaeological Journal, 65 (1970), p. 5.

Berkshire Book, The 107 (1951), 2nd ed., first published 1939. Reading: The Berkshire Federation of Women's Institutes.

Boyd, A.K.(1948), *The History of Radley College 1847-1947*. London: Mowbray.

Bradley, R., R.A. Chambers & C.E. Halpin (1984), *Barrow Hills, Radley 1983-4 Excavations: an Interim Report*. Oxford: Oxford Archaeological Unit.

Buckle, David (1999), *Hostilities Only*. Oxford: Robert Dugdale.

Catchpole, T. M., & H.M.E. Cardwell (1966), 'The Cottage', *The Radleian* (Radley College magazine), No. 663, pp. 322-3.

Chambers, R.A. (1984), 'The Roman Burials', in Bradley, Chambers and Halpin.

Clarke, Helen (1987), 'Agriculture in Late Anglo-Saxon England', in *Domesday* (1987), pp. 43-47.

Cox, Mieneke (1986), *The Story of Abingdon, Part I, 150,000,000 B.C. - 1186 A.D.* Abingdon.

Cox, Mieneke (1989), *Medieval Abingdon 1186-1556 – The Story of Abingdon, Part II*. Abingdon.

Cox, Mieneke (1999), *Abingdon: an 18th Century Country Town – The Story of Abingdon, Part IV*. Abingdon: M. Cox.

DNB (1985) = *The Dictionary of National Biography*, Vol. I. Oxford: Oxford University Press.

Domesday (1987) = *Domesday Book Studies*. London: Alecto Historical Editions, 1987.

Domesday (1988) = *The Berkshire Domesday,* text trans. F.W. Ragg in *Victoria County History Berkshire* (1906). London: Alecto Historical Editions, 1988.

Drysdale, Patrick (1985), *Radley - Ancient Barrows to Modern Parish*. Oxford.

Dyer, Christopher (1994), *Everyday Life in Medieval England*. London & Rio Grande: The Hambledon Press.

Eddershaw, David (1995), *The Civil War in Oxfordshire*. Stroud: Alan Sutton.

Field, The Rev T., (1912), *The Radley District: Its History, Botany, Entomology and Geology*. Oxford: Parker.

Gelling, Margaret (1974), *The Place-Names of Berkshire,* Pt. II, English Place-Name Society, Vol. XL. Cambridge: Cambridge University Press.

Godfrey, J. (1974), 'The Emergence of the Village Church in Anglo-Saxon England', in Rowley (1974), pp. 131-138.

Goudie, A.S., & M.G. Hart (1975), 'Pleistocene Events and Forms in the Oxford Region', in Smith & Scargill, pp. 1-13.

Hammond, Nigel (1974), *Rural Life in the Vale of the White Horse 1780-1914*. West Hanney, Oxon.: Rectory Orchard Books; new edition 1993.

Hearne, Thomas (1918), *Remarks and Collections of Thomas Hearne*, ed. C.E. Doble and others. Oxford: Clarendon Press, 1885-1921.

Hibbert, Christopher & Edward (1988), *The Encyclopaedia of Oxford*. London: Macmillan; Papermac Edition 1992.

Hibbert, Christopher (1997), *No Ordinary Place: Radley College and the Public School System*. London: John Murray.

Hinton, David A. (1967), 'A Cruck House at Lower Radley, Berkshire', *Oxoniensia* 32, pp. 13-33.

Holgate, Robin (1986), 'Mesolithic, Neolithic and Earlier Bronze Age Settlement Patterns S.W. of Oxford', *Oxoniensia*, 51, pp.1-13.

Huntingford, J.W.B. (1925), 'Notes on the History and Antiquities of the Parish of Radley', *Berkshire, Buckinghamshire and Oxfordshire Archaeological Journal*, 29, pp. 137-152.

Jarvis, M.G. (1973), *Soils of the Wantage & Abingdon District*, p 7. The Soil Survey, Rothamsted Experimental Station, Harpenden, Herts.

Jones, G., G. Wallace & W. Skellington (1979), 'Abingdon, Oxfordshire, *Council for British Archaeology, Group 9 Newsletter*, 9, p. 8.

Jowitt, R.L.P. (1950), *Berkshire and Oxfordshire. Penguin Guides*. Harmondsworth: Penguin Books.

Leeds, E. Thurlow (1931), *The Antiquaries Journal*, 11, pp. 399-404.

Loyn, H.R. (1987), 'A General Introduction to Domesday Book', in *Domesday* (1987), pp.1-21.

Martin, G.H. (1987), 'Eleventh-Century Communications', in *Domesday* 1987), (pp. 61-64.

Miles, D. (1976), 'Excavations at Sugworth Farm, Radley', *Oxoniensia,* 41, pp. 6-11.

Miles, David (1974), 'Abingdon & Region: Early Anglo-Saxon Settlement Evidence', in Rowley (1974), pp. 36-41.

Miles David, ed. (1986), *Archaeology at Barton Court Farm, Abingdon, Oxon.* London: Council for British Archaeology, Research Rep. 50; Oxford: Oxford Archaeological Unit Rep. 3.

Morgan, Kenneth O., ed. (1984, rev. 1992), *The Oxford Illustrated History of Britain*. Oxford, New York: Oxford University Press.

Oxoniensia, 35 (1972), Notes and News, p. 104.

Pevsner, Nikolaus (1966), *The Buildings of England: Berkshire*. Harmondsworth: Penguin Books.

Preston Papers, Collected by A.E. Preston, held at Berkshire Records Office.

Radleian, The (c 1969-72). Radley College Magazine.

Rosevear, Alan (1995), *Roads Across the Upper Thames Valley: 7, Turnpike roads Through Abingdon* [n.d.]; *8, Turnpike roads Around Oxford* (1994, rev. 1995). Wantage: Wessex Press.

Rowley, Trevor (1974), ed., *Anglo-Saxon Settlement & Landscape: Papers presented to a Symposium, Oxford 1973.* Oxford: British Archaeological Reports 6.

Salway, Peter (1984), 'Roman Britain', in Morgan.

Sherrat, A. (1986), 'The Radley Earrings Revised', *Oxford Journal of Archaeology*, 5, pp. 61-67; (1987) 'Earrings Again', *Ibid.,* 6, p. 119.

Skeat, W.W. (1911), *The Place-Names of Berkshire.* Oxford: Clarendon Press.

Slack, Paul (1985), *The Impact of Plague in Tudor and Stuart England.* Oxford: Clarendon Press.

Smith, C.G., & D.I. Scargill (1975), *Oxford and Its Region, Geographical Essays.* Oxford: Oxford University Press.

Stenton, F.M. (1913), *The Early History of the Abbey of Abingdon.* Reading: University College; reprinted as Paul Watkins Medieval Studies No. 3. Stamford, Lincs.

Taylor, Christopher (1974), 'The Anglo-Saxon Countryside', in Rowley (1974), pp. 5-15.

Thacker, Fred S. (1920), *The Thames Highway: a History of the Locks and Weirs.* Kew: Fred S. Thacker; republished as *The Thames Highway, Vol. II, Locks and Weirs.* Newton Abbot: David & Charles, 1968.

Thirsk, Joan (1967), 'The Agricultural, Economic, and Social Background to the Diffusion of New Crops, 1500-1700', in *The Agrarian History of England and Wales, Vol. 4, 1500-1640,* ed. Joan Thirsk, general editor H.P.R. Finsberg. Cambridge: Cambridge University Press.

Thomas, R. (1978), 'Three Bronze Age Implements from the River Thames', *Oxoniensia*, 43, pp. 246-8.

Townsend, J. (1910), *A History of Abingdon.* London: Henry Froude; republished 1970 by S.R. Publishers.

Trevelyan, G.M. (1942), *English Social History: A Survey of Six Centuries, Chaucer to Queen Victoria.* London: Longmans, Green.

Trippett, Nigel, & Nicholas de Courtais (1985), *The Abingdon Branch.* Upper Bucklebury, Berks.: Wild Swan Publications.

Tyldesly, Joyce (1983), 'Two Bout Coupé handaxes from Oxfordshire', *Oxoniensia*, 48, p. 149.

VCH, Berks (1924), *The Victoria County History of Berkshire,* Vol. IV, William Page & Rev. P.H. Ditchfield (eds). London: St. Catherine Press, reprinted 1972 by Dawsons of Pall Mall for the Institute of Historical Research.

VCH, Oxon (1979), *The Victoria County History of Oxford,* Vol.IV, Alan Crossley (ed). Oxford & London: Oxford University Press, for the Institute of Historical Research.

Vincent, J.E. (1931), *Highways and Byways in Berkshire.* London: Macmillan.

Wallis, Jeff (1981), 'Abingdon peripheral road', *Council for British Archaeology, Group 9 Newsletter,* 11, p. 134.

Wallis Jeff, (1981), 'Radley: Thrupp Farm', *Council for British Archaeology, Group 9 Newsletter,* 11, pp. 134-7.

Wallis Jeff (1981), 'Radley: Tuckwell's Pit,', *Council for British Archaeology, Group 9 Newsletter,* 11, p. 137.

Wilson, Bob (1997) 'Aspects of Animal Life and Death in an Iron Age Settlement at Tuckwell's Pit', *Oxoniensia,* 62, p. 313.

Wood, Anthony (1891), *The Life and Times of Anthony Wood, described by himself.* Collected from his diaries and other papers by A. Clark (5 volumes, 1891-1900), Vol. 1. Oxford: Oxford University Press.

Index

A

A34 By-pass 2
Abbendune 19
Abbey Fishponds Nature Reserve 7, 34, 104
Abbun, Hill of 19
Abingdon 10, 16, 18, 22, 25-7, 32, 34, 48, 52, 60-2, 64, 69, 71, 73-5, 87, 90, 92-3, 95-8, 104; --Archaeological & Historical Society 12; Ballards 97; --Borough 69; branch railway71, 73, 93, 105; brewers 84; brewery 97; by-pass 105; civil war headquarters 52; Clock House 64-5; fairs 33; Guildhall 69; lock 48, 56; markets 33; members of Parliament 56; mill 45; municipal collection 34; Roysse's school 62; --Rural District Council 95; St. Helen's church 37, 45, 52, 61-2; St. Nicholas church 62; Stratton House 64; townspeople 34; turnpike roads 60-1; Twickenham House 65; Vicar of 79; --Ware 6; weir 45
Abingdon Abbey 7, 19-20, 22, 25-7, 29-34, 37, 41, 45, 74, 78; abbot 26-7, 29-33, 35, 37, 41-3; accounts 34; bailiff 32; Chapel Warden's accounts 34; Chaplain's accounts 34; dissolution 45; fishponds 34, 104; foundation 19; heads of departments 34; manors 30-1, 41; mills 35; Obendientiars 34; Pittancer 34; refounding 19; ruins 19
Alfred the Great 18-20, 22, 28

Ambridge, Charles 73
Amey, Messrs 92
Angles 16
Anglican(ism) 41, 78
Anglo-Saxon(s) 16, 18-20, 23, 27
Aquitaine 29
Aragon, Catherine of 41
Arnold, Matthew 9
Arthur, King 16
Ashmolean Museum 6-7, 9
Asser 20
Athelstan, King 18
Auction Mart (London) 84
Audlett, John 41; Katherine 41
Audlett Drive 87
Aunt Sally 98
Avery(Averie) Henry 54; Joan 51

B

Badcock(e), Anne 49; family 49, 63; Henrie 49; Jane 49; John 65, 76; Simon 49
Badgers Copse 95
Bagley Wood 34, 60, 87
Baines, captain 55
Bakers Close 48, 96
Bakery, The 96, 98
Balgrave Field 49
Ballards of Abingdon 97
Bannister, Amos 97-8
Barley Mow Inn, Clifton Hampden 41
BarrowHills 5-12, 14, 17-8, 104-5; barrow(s) 7, 8, 10, 14; burial site 9
Barton 17-8, 25-7, 29-30, 41, 49, 60; --Court 41, 43, 56, 71, 74; – Court Farm 5, 7, 13, 90; -- Farm 90, 104; estates 27; manor 22, 31, 41-2; villa14, 17
Bayworth 26, 41, 60-1, 77; manor 63, 87

Beaker(s) 7-10; burial(s) 7-9; pots 13; variations 8
Beckett, David 103-4
Bede, the Venerable 16, 18-19
Beeching, Dr. 93
Benson 27
Berkshire 16, 18, 20, 22, 25, 31-2, 36, 61, 67, 87, 98; Berks 105; -- Downs 23; --Records Office 35, 45; Sheriff of 56
Berkshire, Buckinghamshire & Oxfordshire Wildlife Trust 7
Berroc 20
Besselsleigh 56
Big Wood Camp 95; --Park 96
Bishop(s) 25, 79; of Oxford 100; --Transcripts 51
Black Bridge 73, 91, 96
Black Death 30
Blacknall, William 45
Blake 52; Blake's Oak 53
Blenheim Palace 63; --Park 63, 65
Boars Hill 19, 60
Boat Race, Oxford and Cambridge 89
Bodleian Library 48
Bodley, Sir Thomas 48
Borrowsley 30
Bowgrave Field 49
Bowgrove 49
Bowler, William 77
Bowyer(s) 59, 62; Bowyer/Stonhouse alliance 69; estate 84, 90, 97; family 69, 71, 77, 79; George 71; George (Admiral Sir) 69-70; George (Sir) 61, 69-70, 77-80; Mary 80; – sale 71, 85; Sir William, Bart. 69; -- Vase 69; vault 79
Bowyer Arms public house 82, 84, 97-8
Boxford 31

Boxing Day 82
Boyle, Robert 59
Britain 4-5, 8-9, 11-12, 16, 60
British Museum 7
Bronze Age 5-7, 9-11, 13, 17, 105
Brown, Lancelot 'Capability' 65
Brownies 106
Buckinghamshire 69
Bunk, The 73
Burials Register(s) 52, 55-6
Butler, Richard 43; William 42-3

C

Cabin 82
Cadwalla 19
Caesar, Julius 12
Cambridge 23, 89
Cameron Avenue 5
Carfax 66; --Conduit 66
Carter, William 52
Celtic 11-13, 20, 23; -- Christianity 19
Celts 12
Census 1801 63, 71; 1851 80; 1871 75; 1881 71; 1901 87, 97; 1911 87; 1981 87; 1991 87
Chandlings --Farm 43, 90; --School 87
Charles I 46, 52, 56
Chaundpool 43
Chestnuts 105
Chicksands 42
Chilswell 19
Christ in Glory 102
Christianity 28
Christmas 82; Day 82
Church 19, 29, 103; --Army Sisters 94; --Farm 67, 80, 90; --Road 48, 59, 73, 97; --Room 103
Churchill, John 63
Cissa 19
Civil War 37, 46, 52-3, 56, 60-1, 80

Claudius 12
Clifton Hampden 41`
Close, The 82, 93
Club -- Bingo 106; --Cricket 106;
--Darby and Joan 106; --History
105, 106; --Men's Football 106;
--Men's and Women's Fellowship
106; Social 106; --Swimming 106
Cologne 79
Commission 33
Commons, House of 56
Community of the Resurrection 79
Comptroller of the Royal Household
63
Conduit 66
Conservation Area 94
Council sites 95
Coventry canal 61
Croke, Thomas 33
Cromwell 56, 58
Crouch family 51; Walter 51
Cruch family 49; Martin 49, 54;
William 49
Crusade 29
Cubs 106
Culham 31
Cumnor 26, 31
Curtis 92; --Gravel Pits 97; --J. & Sons
97

D

Daisy Bank 34; --Fen 7
Danes 18-19, 28
Darby and Joan Club 106
Dawson's Cottage 93
de Chereburk, John 30
de Clifford, John 37
de Frilford, Henry 33
de Hynton, Thomas 30

Deane, Elizabeth 49; family 49; Joan
51; John, 51; Thomas 49, 51
Denham 69; --Court 69
Didcot 71; --Power Station 92
Diocese, Chancellor of 102
Dissolution 29-30, 41, 43, 45-6, 58
Dockar, William 76-7
Dockar-Drysdale, Josephine 77, 90,
100; Mrs. 82, 84
Domesday 18, 21, 23, 25-9
Dorchester 19
Doyley, Anne 42; Elizabeth 42; John
42; Katherine 42; Margery 42
Drayton 37
Dry Sandford 37
Drysdale Close 95
Dukes Cut 61
Dutch 46; --Elm Disease 91

E

Eason Drive 105
Easter 31
*Ecclesiastical History of the English
People* 19
Edgemead 54
Education Act 1870 80
Edward VI 42
Edward, King (the Confessor) 26
Eight Acre Field 11
Elizabeth I, Queen 42-3, 104
Elizabeth II, Queen 94, 100
Elizabeth, Princess 42
England 6, 16, 18-20, 23, 25, 28-9, 41,
58, 104
English 16, 20, 32, 41, 58; -- Civil War
56
Essex, Earl of 52, 54
Europe 11, 30, 56, 60

O

Orchard, the 73
Ordric, Abbot of Abingdon 35
Oxford 7, 13, 23, 25, 29, 34-5, 40, 42,
48-9, 52, 59-61, 63-7, 71, 74-5, 89-
90, 96-8, 100, 102; --Archaeolog-
ical Unit 39, 105; -- Road 87;
--University 61
Oxford and Cambridge Boat Race 89
Oxfordshire 87, 98; High Sheriff of 46;
Oxonia Bakery 97

P

Palaeolithic 4
Paris, Matthew 32
Parish Council 91; magazine 79, 89
Park End 48; --Farm 48, 59, 67, 90, 96-
7
Parliament 41, 52, 54; Long 56, 58
Parr, Catherine 42
Parsons, Jack 98
Peachcroft 14, 64, 67, 87, 90-91;
--Farm 96, 105
Peacock --Cottages 48; --Tree 93
Peasants' Revolt 30
Pebble Hill 95-96
Peisley, Bartholomew 63
Perrin, H. 61
Philip I, King of France 29
Picts 16
Pixell, Rev. J.V. 89, 106
Place, The 49, 54
Pleistoscene 1
Pocock 63
Pond Head 5
Pooke Eyot 35
Porter 35; Porter's Eyot 35
Preston Papers 77
Protector, Lord 42; Protectorate 46

Pumney 2, 27, 41, 48, 67, 90; --Farm 4,
74, 96

Q

Queen's Court 100

R

Radcliffe, John 37
Radley 1-3, 5-7, 10, 15, 17, 19-20,
22-6, 29-30, 32, 34-5, 37-8, 41- 3,
45-6, 48-9, 52-6, 58-67, 69, 71,
73-5, 78-80, 82, 84, 86-7, 89-92,
95-6, 98, 100, 102-5, 106;
Band of Hope 82; Boxing Day 82;
Cabin, the 82; Close, The 82, 93:
Christmas Day 82; Feast 82; Guy
Fawkes Night 82; Harvest Home
82; History Club 105, 106; Large
Wood 34, 87, 95-6, 105; Lower
Radley 2, 8, 22, 27, 39, 41, 48, 63,
67, 73-4, 82, 89-90, 92-4, 96-7;
manor of 42-3, 46, 49, 52, 63; May
Day 82; newsagent/village store 97;
--Oak 105; parish boundary 87-9;
parish registers 45, 49, 53, 55, 63;
post office 94, 97; Pre-school 104;
pond 74, 80, 93; public house 97;
--Road 34; school 80, 82-3, 104;
school house 104; sports pavilion
94; smithy 80; --Station 71-4, 84,
92-3; station master 73; Survey of
71; village green 93; Terrier 49-50,
54; Tithe Award 71; Tithe Map 93;
village hall 94-5, 104; village
organisations 106; Women's
Institute 106
Radley Church 2, 15, 19, 35, 37, 45-6,
51-3, 56, 61-3, 69, 73, 79-82, 97,
100, 102-104; aisle 36, 53, 61, 79,
103; altar tomb 53; arcade 36;